From Easter Week *to* Flanders Field

The Diaries and Letters of John Delaney SJ, 1916-1919

Thomas Morrissey SJ

First published in 2015
by Messenger Publications

ISBN 978-19102481-1-9

Messenger Publications,
37 Lower Leeson Street, Dublin 2
www.messenger.ie

Designed by Messenger Publications Design Department
Printed by Naas Printing Ltd

John Delaney SJ

Table of Contents

We have loved him in life, let us not forget him in death St. Ambrose.

✝

In Loving Memory of

Rev. John Delaney, S.J.

St. Francis Xaviers,
Gardiner Street Upper, Dublin

WHO DIED

On the 8th August, 1956

AGED 73 YEARS

R. I. P.

O GOD, Who didst raise to the dignity of the Priesthood Thy servant, JOHN, grant we beseech Thee, that he may be admitted to the eternal fellowship of Thy Apostles through Christ our Lord.

Acknowledgements

This book has been in preparation, on and off, for some three to four years. Acknowledgements of sources have been made at the end of each chapter, but I take this opportunity to express my personal thanks to a variety of people and institutions. First, as for all my books, I wish to express my gratitude for the on-going support and encouragement of my provincial, Fr Tom Layden; to my tolerant and supportive Jesuit Community at Manresa House, Clontarf; to Frs John Looby and Bill Toner; and to Fr Fergus O'Donoghue as reader and adviser in this as in so many other books.

More immediately, in relation to the preparation of this biography, my thanks are due to the efficient and helpful staff of the National Archives of Ireland and of the National Library. With this work and several others, I am indebted to Mary Glennon and June Rooney, and the other most able and helpful members of the Milltown Park Jesuit Library. Many hours have been spent in the Irish Jesuit Archives, and much of this work is due to the assistance and supportive knowledge of Damien Burke, the Assistant-Archivist.

Further afield, the book has been greatly helped by the assistance of John de Silva, Australian editor of 'The Aloyisian' magazine, who unearthed many letters of Delaney written from the front in 1917–1918. For the life of John Delaney in the Belgian province, great assistance has come from Patricia Quaghebour and Jo Luyton, who kindly and patiently searched the archives of the Flemish Jesuit Province, deposited in the Kadoc Archief van de Vlamse, Louvain; and for John Delaney as chaplain a great deal has depended on the expertise of Stephen Bellis, an authority on chaplains in the British armed forces during two World Wars, who most generously provided information from the Downside Abbey Archives and from the British Public Record Office.

At Manresa House, may I register thanks once more to the office staff, who have always been most resourceful in copying material. Finally, I offer a very special word of appreciation to Cecilia West, Sarah Brady, and Paula Nolan, and all the courteous and highly professional staff of Messenger Publications. They have been a joy to work with, and the production and design of the book speaks for itself.

Preview

John Delaney influenced many people but left scarcely any mark in recorded history. His life was a varied one, spent in many places, and experiencing major events in Ireland and Europe. He was born into a Dublin working-class family on 4 July 1883. At the age of sixteen he moved to Limerick to study for the priesthood. Some years later, he became a Jesuit in Belgium before going to work in Ceylon.

He returned to Dublin in 1913, the year of the great strike/lock-out, and stayed until 1917. During the Easter Week insurrection, 1916, he walked from one point of military activity to another, chronicling all he saw. The following year he was appointed military chaplain, served in France and Flanders, 1917–1919, and was decorated with the Military Cross for outstanding bravery and dedication to his men.

Following the war, he returned to Ceylon. When his health broke down eleven years later, he came back to Dublin. With renewed energy he threw himself into the work of the Jesuit mission staff, who gave retreats and parish missions throughout Ireland. Before long, he was greatly in demand. His endless response to the demands made on him eventually resulted in a further break down in health. His final years were spent, most of them very actively, in Gardiner Street Church, Dublin. He died in 1956.

Delaney's diary on day to day events during Easter Week 1916, and his various letters from the Front in 1917 and 1918, may be of interest to readers in Australia, Belgium, Great Britain, Ceylon, and the United States of America as well as in Ireland.

Chapter One

BIRTH TO ORDINATION, 1883–1916

John was one of eight children – two boys and six girls – born to Michael and Maria (nee Cunningham) Delaney. The family lived at 13 Charleville Mall, Strand Road, Dublin, one of a number of houses overlooking the Royal Canal. That waterway with its traffic of barges, its swans, fishing, and swimming on hot summer days, offered much to interest growing boys. The census returns for 1901 described John's father as a 'coachman'. Nothing is recorded of the family atmosphere apart from the implication that the parents were practising Catholics. John was educated for eight years by the Christian Brothers at O'Connell's Schools. After his intermediate examination, he expressed his intention to become a Catholic priest. He faced a real obstacle, however, in that his family had not the money to pay for his training in a diocesan seminary. He solved the problem by applying for entry to the Apostolic School, situated at the Jesuit-run Mungret College, some four miles west of Limerick city.

At Mungret College

The Apostolic School was set up by a Jesuit priest, William Ronan (1825–1907)[1], to cater for young men who wished to become priests but had not the financial means required for attendance at diocesan seminary colleges. Students at the Apostolic School were financed largely

© Irish Jesuit Archives

MUNGRET COLLEGE, LIMERICK

by bursaries from bishops with dioceses in English-speaking countries outside Ireland. The bishops, in turn, expected their protégés to devote their lives to working in the bishops' dioceses. Many of the past students worked in North America and Britain, some in Australasia, India/Ceylon, South Africa, and even South America and China. The students' choice of diocese usually occurred while they were studying at Mungret.

Students at the Apostolic School were prepared for the matriculation examination of the Royal University of Ireland. Subsequently, they were able to sit for a BA examination at the college. John Delaney entered Mungret in 1899. He appears to have settled in well and to have worked hard. Two years were given to studying philosophy and other subjects in preparation for the matriculation. He was one of eight students sitting for the examination. All were successful. They then commenced the First Arts course. In this, seven obtained honours, including John, and one passed.[2] All were successful in the second year examinations. In 1904, John was one of the five graduates. The *Mungret Annual*, 1905, carried photographs of 'Our graduates of the Apostolic School, 1904', bedecked in gown and mortar board. After each name, in brackets, the mission was indicated for which each was destined. Thus: 'John Croke, BA (China), John Delaney, BA (Ceylon), Richard Judge, BA (Eastern Missions), William Griffin, BA (Capetown), and John Cullen, BA (Tasmania)'.

From time to time visiting prelates addressed the Apostolic School students, encouraging them to join their particular mission. John Delaney was attracted by the Belgian Jesuit bishop of Ceylon, Dr Joseph Van Reeth, who had come to Ireland to enlist English-speaking priests and clerical students for a college in his diocese of Galle, in the island of Ceylon. Among those who responded to his invitation was the principal of St Ignatius College, Galway, Fr Denis Murphy SJ (1862–1943). Under Murphy's tactful and capable management, the school in Galle developed from a collection of huts, where boys were taught the elements of reading, writing and arithmetic, to a secondary school of distinction, St Aloysius College, where pupils were prepared for the senior school Cambridge Certificate. In 1922, after twenty years in Galle, Murphy was compelled, for reasons of health, to return to Ireland.[3] John Delaney was to serve under him as a scholastic and later to succeed him as headmaster.

At Mungret, Delaney was attracted both to Ceylon and the Jesuits. As the Irish Jesuits did not have a mission in Ceylon, he solved the dual attraction by joining the Belgian Jesuit province, which had a mission in southern Ceylon in the diocese of Galle. John joined the Jesuit novitiate at Tronchiennes (now, Drongen) Belgium, on 24 September, 1904. He was 21 years of age.

Before continuing his story, it will help towards a better understanding of him to dwell on aspects of his life at Mungret. The students of the Apostolic School were encouraged to organise and participate in a variety of activities. These included team sports, athletics and boating, as well as dramatic productions, debating, historical and cultural societies, special outings, and the publication of an annual. Delaney received only one mention in the *Mungret Annual* for participation in team games. This referred to his being a member of the Apostolics' soccer team in a game against Crescent College, Limerick.[4] His main physical activity was in athletics. The *Annual* for Christmas 1900 recorded that J. Delaney (off 4 yards) won the 220 yards race for the Junior Apostolics (the pre-matriculation students), and (off 8 yards) was second to John Croke in the 440 yards event. In the 880 yards (off scratch), however, he came first.[5] Among the attractions during his first Christmas vacation at Mungret were paper chases. 'John Delaney and William Griffin were the hares on one occasion but the enjoyment was marred by a heavy fall of snow. J. Delaney and J. Croke led the boys a good run over splendid country on another occasion.' Delaney continued his athletic activity in succeeding years. His energy in that field was to be much appreciated when he arrived in Ceylon.

In his first year in Mungret, Delaney was impressed by the widespread interest in Irish history and culture, which was reflected in the visits to places of historical and geographical significance and were recorded on camera and commented on in the college annual. Every effort appears to have been made to broaden the interests and experiences of the students. The *Mungret Annual* of January 1904 made reference to concerts, outings, visiting lecturers to the college, and skating on nearby Lough Mór [6]. As summer approached there was boating and swimming in the River Shannon. The students had access to the river through the estate of Lord Emly, a patron of the college. There were also outings further afield, to Galway and to Kilkee: travelling to Foynes and from there by steamer to Kilrush, whence they were carried on the West Clare Railway to their destination.

Delaney participated in the concerts and dramatic productions presented by the apostolic sudents. The experience was to prove helpful in his dealings with pupils in Ceylon and with soldiers in France. On 3 December 1903, Delaney was recorded as appearing with some distinction in *Soggart Aroon*: 'John Delaney is deserving of special mention for his admirable presentation of Irish peasant life'[7]. Subsequently, the jubilee issue of the *Mungret Annual, 1882–1907*, described *Soggarth Aroon* as an excellent play, written by Rev. F. Connell SJ. 'It was a serio-comic play, the subject for which centres round the tyranny of an Irish landlord of the nineteenth century.' Delaney also played one of the slaves in Cardinal Wiseman's *The Hidden Glen*. Earlier in 1903, in the celebrations to mark St Patrick's Day, he was a member of the choir in the concert arranged for the occasion. On Easter Monday, when there was a dramatisation of the history of the Irish Brigade, with individual items of music and song, J. Delaney sang 'Clare's Dragoons'[8]. In his final year at Mungret, he played Macduff in Shakespeare's *Macbeth*. Significantly, it was observed that he 'displayed all that energy of character that made him so suitable for the part'[9].

Saint Aloysius' College, Ceylon

From Belgium to Ceylon

At the end of two years at Tronchiennes, in September 1906, John took vows of poverty, chastity and obedience in the Society of Jesus. He stayed at Tronchiennes for a further year. The year was devoted to guided study in the Arts, which increased his grasp of Latin, French and English literature. Later, Jesuit records would indicate that he spoke Irish in addition to French and English. He spent 1907–08 at Louvain studying philosophy. He did well, scoring marks of 4 out of 5.[10]

Meantime, Bishop Van Reeth, who had attracted Delaney to Ceylon, was continuing to foster the development of education in his diocese.

On 12 April 1907, he congratulated the superior of the Jesuit mission on the success achieved by St Aloysius College in the Cambridge examinations, adding : 'The two Irishmen, who entered the Society for the mission of Galle, constitute a good attachment to our mission'.[11] Six weeks later, on 25 May, he informed the Jesuit provincial in Belgium that he had visited 'our two Irishmen' at Tronchiennes, Charles Piler (who had been in Mungret also) and John Delaney, who, he reiterated, would be 'two good acquisitions for the college'.[12] In a letter to the provincial the following year, 14 December 1908, Van Reeth indicated the difficulty of life on the mission. Fr Van Austin had to leave. Fr Schafer was *hors de combat*. Many of the others were not more than demi-men so far as work was concerned. On a more positive note, however, he reported that the Apostolic Delegate was greatly impressed by the number of conversions and baptisms in the mission. In 1907–08 there were 925 baptisms, of which 392 were adult converts.[13]

There was a positive note also in an informative letter sent by the headmaster of St Aloysius College, Fr Murphy, to Mungret with a view to encouraging applicants for the Ceylon Mission:[14]

> We need English, or still better, Irish, aid very badly here, especially for college work. We have now a nice college of some 300 dusky lads – and myself the only Paddy! We have white boys, chiefly of Dutch descent, called Burgers, and yellow boys – Singhalese and Portuguese – with many black boys of Tamil blood. The latter are industrious when made to be, and by nature very gentle and obedient. The Eastern memory is very good. The mind is acute but lacks reasoning power. All these qualities of mind and character are improving under European education.

Continuing his depiction of school life in the college for which John Delaney was destined, Murphy commented:

> Lying and theft seem second nature to young and old here – quite shocking at first. But our boys quickly learn that "honesty is the best policy" in word and deed; so I find them now truthful and honest when they find both esteemed and rewarded; while the opposite being punishment and disgrace. Amongst my 300 boys I have not had for many months a complaint of loss of books [stolen] which was quite a plague formerly. Our Catholic boys have much piety.

St Aloysius' College crest

The account went on:

> At games we do well. The college holds the championship for football over the Buddhist, Anglican, and Wesleyan colleges – past and present. The Aloysian club holds the football championship of Galle… Of course all this makes our lads proud of their college, and fosters *esprit de corps*. The evenings are quite cool enough for Association [football]; but Rugby cannot flourish in the tropics.

Murphy concluded: 'I like the Ceylon climate better than Ireland's. We have no winter, nor is the heat too great; a fresh land or sea breeze constantly blows. I hope some more will come to us from Mungret. The East has greatest need of English speakers.'

The *Mungret Apostolic Record* noted that prior to his departure for Ceylon, John Delaney returned to Ireland, August 1908, to spend a few days with his parents. During that time he visited Mungret. Subsequently, he spent a pleasant day with Mungret friends in Panningen, Holland. The *Apostolic Record* further observed: 'We hear from time to time of his work in Ceylon and of the cheerful spirit which always accompanied him. He now fills Rev. Mr. Piler's SJ, place in Galle College. Mr. Piler is finishing his philosophy in India'.

St Aloysius College problems and progress

Denis Murphy's letter on school life in St Aloysius College omitted occasions of disharmony. On arrival in Galle, Delaney found himself in a college where there was disunity among the Jesuits. The Belgian Fathers had founded the college in 1895. They now, it appears, felt threatened by the assurance and assertiveness of the 'English' in matters educational. Thus, the superior of St Aloysius, Fr Olivier Feron, wrote to the Belgian provincial, on 15 March 1909: 'our two Irish priests don't like the superior [of the mission]. They are very English and not able to enter into our ways; our mentality is not theirs'. They had a different way of assessing matters. This was due 'to a training completely different from ours'.[15] On 6 April, Feron complained that the three Irish/English men were always together at table and 'always occupied with English ideas ... It is the utopia of the Empire that the English are going to input into our plan'.[16] In the same vein he commented on 25 May 1909, that in St Aloysius College they never had 'a free moment'. Lodgings were poor, they were debilitated by the heat, but the main ground for concern was the 'absence of union between the English and the Belgians'. 'I say English', he continued, because although John Delaney is Irish he 'is forced to be as English as the English by blood. Their opinion is that the Belgians understand nothing about education. Our directions are not to be followed'.[17]

By the end of the year, Rev. Feron was able to report 'our boarding school is improving. There is a good spirit in it'. The plan for the building of the new college had been drawn up, though a site had not yet been established.[18] At the same time, he was still uneasy about the 'English' approach to education:

> The English scholastics [Jesuits previous to ordination] seem to forget their true role here. We are not at Galle to convert the Singhalese to English ideas, which are always more or less like Protestantism, but to form Christians. Sports, exams are all very well, but above all we are to be ministers of the Gospel. The Irish are not like the Irish in Ireland: here they are more English than the English themselves.[19]

Despite the concerns of Fr Feron, Delaney managed to make a positive impression at the college. During 1911, Joseph Shiel SJ, Shemlaganar, India, observed: 'Mr. Delaney is doing splendid work in Galle, Ceylon.

Saint Aloysius' College, Galle

His cheery character has won for him the name of "Joyous Delaney".'The cheeryness survived the death of John's father in the spring of 1911.[20]

Scholastics in the British/Irish schools played a vital role. Not only were they active in teaching, they also took a lively part in extra-curricular activities involving pupils – in various sports, debating, drama, and a variety of clubs and societies. They had far more energy than the priests on the staff, and they were nearer in age to their pupils, and hence could get to know them well. The impression conveyed by Fr Feron's letters is that the role of the scholastic in Belgian, and perhaps French, tradition was less physically active. In the event, the role played by Delaney in Galle met with much public approval. This is indicated by newspaper comment on the occasion of his leaving Ceylon to pursue his theological studies in Ireland.

Two newspaper cuttings from un-named Ceylonise papers, which are preserved in the Irish Jesuit Archives,[21] manifest how highly he was regarded. The shorter account observed that it was due to his efforts 'that sports, the cadets, and the Boy Scouts of the college were brought to an efficient standing'. He would be greatly missed by the college as well as by 'the general Catholic community with whom he was very popular'. As he left for Ireland to complete his studies, several group photographs were taken of him with the college staff, the Cambridge forms, and the members of the College Sports Club. 'The Galle Catholic Club, too, read an address to him and presented him some valuable Ceylon curios; and, last but not least, the St Mary's Society, with its president, Rev. Father A.N. Fernando, also honoured the departing Father with an address and a group photograph.'

The longer account, which also mistakenly termed him 'Father', elaborated on the tributes at his departure for Ireland. Of the 'farewell function' at the Catholic Club, it related: 'the entertainment was in the form of a "social evening" on the club grounds. Refreshments were lavishly served and the greatest conviviality prevailed. Brother Verbingen with his little fife and drum band enlivened the day's proceedings'. The Hon Vice-President of the Club, Mr. P. Anandappa, spoke of 'the sterling qualities of Father Delaney and handed him a fine collection of Ceylon curios as a souvenir of his short stay in Gall… Father Delaney, in reply, thanked the Club for their kind appreciation of his services and for their presence and good wishes.' He hoped to be back in Ceylon on the completion of his studies. 'The proceedings terminated with "God Save the King" played by the college band.'

At St Aloysius College there was further recognition. On the opening day of the term after the mid-summer vacation, Delaney was presented by staff and boys with an album of group photographs and an illuminated address that featured, 'besides the college and mission coat of arms, the shamrock, the wolf dog, the harp, the seven churches and the setting sun all emblematic of the Emerald Isle…' The superior of the college, the previously concerned Rev. Fr O. Feron, addressed the assembled school with laudatory words for Mr. Delaney and expressed the hope that he would return to Galle.

That Delaney was sent back to Ireland for theological studies, rather than to Belgium, was linked to the views of Bishop Van Reeth and Fr Veut, superior of the Jesuit mission, that as Mr. Delaney had a BA from Dublin he might progress to an MA while there, 'to the great advantage of the college'.[22]

© Irish Jesuit Archives

A GROUP OF PAST MUNGRET STUDENTS AT MILLTOWN PARK, DUBLIN
Back Row: Rev. T. Maher SJ; Rev. M. Saul SJ; Rev. H. Johnston SJ
Front Row: Rev. P. McCartney SJ; Rev. J. Croke SJ; Rev. J. Delaney SJ

Back in Ireland

In the autumn of 1913, John Delaney arrived at Milltown Park Theologate, Sandford Road, Dublin, to commence his years of studies prior to ordination to the priesthood. He lived in the Jesuit community there from 1913 to 1917. He arrived at a time of considerable upheaval in the country. The long-awaited expectation of Home Rule was being opposed by armed unionist volunteers in Ulster. In Dublin there was a strike/lock out in the autumn and winter of 1913, which divided and disrupted the city. The following year was marked by the passing of an attenuated Home Rule Bill that was then deferred until after the world war. The ravages of the war dominated the news in 1915. In the following year, an unexpected insurrection took place in Dublin during Easter Week. It was to have an enduring impact and, as will appear, it greatly preoccupied John Delaney.

During his years in Milltown, two semi-public actions of his were recorded. Both during 1914. The *Irish Catholic*, 11 April 1914, carried a letter from 'The Rev. Delaney SJ.' who had spent 'several years' in Ceylon. It was devoted to exposing a calumny on the Jesuit mission in Chota, Nagpur, India, which had appeared in an issue of the mission magazine published in Trinity College, Dublin.[23] Three days before his letter was published, he had visited Mungret College and given an illustrated lecture on the island of Ceylon to the students.

His was one of a series of 'occasional lectures' given by such notable figures as Douglas Hyde, founder of the Gaelic League, and Fr Tom Finlay, co-founder of the Irish Agricultural Cooperative Movement. As a result, he took great care with his talk and choice of slides. Ceylon was two-thirds the size of Ireland, he informed his audience. Then, with the aid of slides, he illustrated the luxurious tropical vegetation and the geographical features of the island, the means of transport, the diversity of its inhabitants, their religious beliefs, and the influence of Christian missionaries. His affection for the island and its people appeared in his relation of stories and legends relating to different locations and customs, not without sardonic wit at times. He remarked that:

> The inhabitants came in every type, from the wild man of the woods to the polished accountant in a government office. There were Dobies, Singalese, Brahmins, Hindus, Malays. The latter gentlemen have an inordinate respect for civic peace, and, consequently, every one of that tribe enters the police force, whose brilliant uniform he dons, leaving, however, the boots severely alone.

The Catholic Church was the most flourishing of the Christian denominations, Delaney claimed. 'Its schools topped the list in all Government examinations.' He spoke about St Aloysius College, which was worked by Jesuits of the Belgian province except for three Irishmen, two of whom were past students of Mungret – Rev. Mr. Piler SJ, and Rev. John Delaney himself. The *Mungret Annual*, July 1914, reporting on the lecture, concluded: 'a number of slides showing the different phases of college life in the Island of India brought a most interesting lecture to a close'.[24]

The absence of further evidence of any public or semi-public activity might reasonably lead a researcher to conclude that John Delaney, after his first year at Milltown, had settled down to a sheltered academic life as he prepared for ordination. His life to date, however, suggested otherwise. He was a man of great energy who was also determined and venturesome: he had sought out Mungret College when he wanted to be a priest, had met a difficult dual objective by joining the Belgian Jesuits and working in Ceylon, and had adapted sufficiently to win over a critical Jesuit superior. In the same venturesome spirit, bolstered by considerable energy, he set out to explore the Easter Rising of 1916 and to keep a day-to-day diary of his experiences. In the process, he displayed an acquaintance with outside events and his share in some of the religious and political prejudices of his time.

NOTES

1. For William Ronan see T.J. Morrissey. *William Ronan SJ, 1825–1907: War Chaplain, Missioner, Founder of Mungret College.* (Dublin: Messenger Publications, 2002)
2. *Mungret Annual,* Christmas 1901, pp. 50, 69
3. *Irish Province News,* 1944, p. 725
4. *Mungret Annual,* Jan 1904, pp. 63, 65
5. Idem, Christmas 1900, p. 58
6. Idem, Jan 1904, p. 56 7 Idem, p. 59. 8. Idem, p. 61 9. Idem, 1905, p. 61
10. Belgian Jesuit Archives (BJA) deposited in Kadoc, Archief van de Vlamse, BE/942855/1595/ relevant file 4642
11. Idem, BE 942855/1595/ file 11541, 028-030
12. Idem, BE 942855/1595/ file 11541, 029
13. Idem, File 11541, 036-037. The information from the Belgian Jesuit Archives has been made available courtesy of the Belgian Jesuits and of Patricia Quaghebeur, Kadoc, Archief van de Vlamse Provincie van de Societeit van Jezus.
14. *Mungret Annual,* July 1908, p. 157
15. Idem, f. 11245, 004-5 16 Idem f. 11245, 033-034
17. Idem, f. 11245, 011-016, p. 3
18. To the provincial, 15 Nov 1909; f. 11245, 038-042
19. 24 Oct 1909. f.11245, 035-037
20. *Mungret Apostolic Record,* Jan 1912, p. 72
21. Irish Jesuit Archives (IJA), John Delaney papers, J29/1(2)
22. J. Van Reeth – Provincial, 31 May 1913; f. 11541, 086-90, esp.087
23. *Mungret Annual,* 1915, p. 106
24. Idem, July 1914, p. 201

POBLACHT NA H EIREANN.

THE PROVISIONAL GOVERNMENT OF THE IRISH REPUBLIC TO THE PEOPLE OF IRELAND.

IRISHMEN AND IRISHWOMEN: In the name of God and of the dead generations from which she receives her old tradition of nationhood, Ireland, through us, summons her children to her flag and strikes for her freedom.

Having organised and trained her manhood through her secret revolutionary organisation, the Irish Republican Brotherhood, and through her open military organisations, the Irish Volunteers and the Irish Citizen Army, having patiently perfected her discipline, having resolutely waited for the right moment to reveal itself, she now seizes that moment, and, supported by her exiled children in America and by gallant allies in Europe, but relying in the first on her own strength, she strikes in full confidence of victory.

We declare the right of the people of Ireland to the ownership of Ireland, and to the unfettered control of Irish destinies, to be sovereign and indefeasible. The long usurpation of that right by a foreign people and government has not extinguished the right, nor can it ever be extinguished except by the destruction of the Irish people. In every generation the Irish people have asserted their right to national freedom and sovereignty; six times during the past three hundred years they have asserted it in arms. Standing on that fundamental right and again asserting it in arms in the face of the world, we hereby proclaim the Irish Republic as a Sovereign Independent State, and we pledge our lives and the lives of our comrades-in-arms to the cause of its freedom, of its welfare, and of its exaltation among the nations.

The Irish Republic is entitled to, and hereby claims, the allegiance of every Irishman and Irishwoman. The Republic guarantees religious and civil liberty, equal rights and equal opportunities to all its citizens, and declares its resolve to pursue the happiness and prosperity of the whole nation and of all its parts, cherishing all the children of the nation equally, and oblivious of the differences carefully fostered by an alien government, which have divided a minority from the majority in the past.

Until our arms have brought the opportune moment for the establishment of a permanent National Government, representative of the whole people of Ireland and elected by the suffrages of all her men and women, the Provisional Government, hereby constituted, will administer the civil and military affairs of the Republic in trust for the people.

We place the cause of the Irish Republic under the protection of the Most High God, Whose blessing we invoke upon our arms, and we pray that no one who serves that cause will dishonour it by cowardice, inhumanity, or rapine. In this supreme hour the Irish nation must, by its valour and discipline and by the readiness of its children to sacrifice themselves for the common good, prove itself worthyof the august destiny to which it is called.

Signed on Behalf of the Provisional Government,

THOMAS J. CLARKE,

SEAN Mac DIARMADA, THOMAS MacDONAGH,
P. H. PEARSE, EAMONN CEANNT,
JAMES CONNOLLY. JOSEPH PLUNKETT.

Chapter 2

A PERSONAL ACCOUNT OF EASTER WEEK 1916

Background

At Milltown Park, the student body was not large, but it was international. In the year ahead of John Delaney there were seventeen students of whom seven were Irish, four English, two Mexican; and there was one each from the United States of America, Canada, Belgium, and Spain. Among the Irish was Frank Browne, who was destined to win honours as an army chaplain and as an outstanding photographer. John was scheduled for ordination to the priesthood on 31 July 1916.[1] During Easter Week of 1916 there were no theology lectures for the Milltown students. This gave John the opportunity to visit his mother and members of his family, and to explore the centres of armed resistance in the city and suburbs. He committed his experiences each day to his diary. The fact that he wore clerical clothes and clerical collar, the usual garb for senior clerical students at the time, almost certainly eased his contact with people and authorities as he moved from place to place.

A great deal has been written about the Easter Rising of 1916, and there have been many personal reminiscences and some diaries. John Delaney's diary contains no significant insights into military or political activity. He was able to move around the city only for the early days before the British reinforcements arrived. Thereafter, he was confined largely to viewing places of conflict in the areas south of the River Liffey.

Some of Delaney's observations regarding activity in those areas, as well as his relation of some experiences of other Jesuits, will be of interest in providing knowledge about certain events, in reflecting the degree of confusion among the populace as to what was happening, and in conveying some of the prejudices of contemporary Dublin Catholics. Social, political and religious attitudes are intermingled and reflected in the way Delaney speaks of certain Protestant unionist ladies, who warmly welcomed the British troops. He, like many Catholic clergy, was much influenced by the vigorous writing of D.P. Moran in his weekly newspaper, *The Leader* (founded 1900). Moran advocated a cultural nationalism based on Catholic and Gaelic values, and urged people to learn the Irish language and purge themselves of the 'West Britishism' that looked to English ways and values. Arthur E. Clery, who wrote for *The Leader,* claimed in an article, 'The Gaelic League, 1893–1919', in *Studies,* September 1919, that Moran's paper had brought practically all the Catholic clergy to the side of the Irish Ireland movement. Moran was pre-eminent in his use of damaging nick-names. Thus, the Anglo-Irish were dubbed 'West Brits', the native Catholic Irish who copied English fashions and ideas were labelled 'Shoneens', and, significantly in Delaney's case, the Protestants/unionists were described as 'Sour Faces'.

John Delaney's overall account is unguardedly personal and baldly honest. It was never intended for publication. No care was taken to avoid repetition, to correct awkwardness of style, or to clarify the meaning of what he had written. The diary commences on Easter Sunday, the day before the insurrection.

The DIARY[2]

Sunday, 23 April

There were posters around the town announcing "No Mobilisation". People asked, what had happened. Why no parades today? There were not even route marches. Something must be wrong. Perhaps the Government forbade all! The papers had a small paragraph – "Owing to the very critical position, all orders given to Irish Volunteers ... are hereby rescinded...". I saw one company marching to Mass. They looked a very respectable set of

Sunday. 24th April. The Posters were around the town
announcing "No Mobilisation" "What had happened?"
people asked. Why no parades today? Not even
Route Marches. Something must be wrong. Perhaps
the Government forbade all!! The papers had a
small paragraph – "Owing to the very critical position
all orders given to Irish Volunteers .... are hereby
rescinded ......" I saw one Company marching to Mass.
They looked a very respectable set of fellows & would
figure well in any army. So Sunday passed
& all that was to have taken place with it. On
Easter Monday, as I went into Town, I met great numbers
of Volunteers all marching towards St. Stephens Green. I
thought they were going to have a Route March, or go off
for some manoeuvres by Harcourt St Station. They were gathering
in from all sides. Some on bikes with very heavy loads,
others carrying very heavy packs practically all had
rifles. People did not mind them as they were so
accustomed to see them march through the City. I
proceeded on my way & went home to 13. Harry

THE FIRST PAGE OF JOHN DELANEY SJ'S SEVENTY-EIGHT PAGE DIARY

The diary starts on Sunday, April 23rd 1916
(incorrectly written as Sunday, 24th April by Delaney)

fellows and would figure well in any army. So Sunday passed and all that was to have taken place with it.

Easter Monday, 24 April

As I went into town, I met great numbers of Volunteers all marching towards St Stephen's Green. I thought they were going to have a route march or go off for some manoeuvres by Harcourt Street [Railway] Station. They were gathering in from all sides. Some on bicycles with very heavy loads, others carrying very heavy packs, practically all had rifles. People did not mind them as they were so accustomed to see them march through the city. I proceeded on my way and went home to 13 [Charleville Mall].

Harry, Johanna,[3] and myself went off to Clontarf after lunch and I was particularly struck by the very small number of people in the trams. On bank holidays they were usually crowded, but today hardly anybody was going to Howth. There was something wrong. We went on 'till we came to St Laurence's Road, where we heard from a man, who had come out from the town, that the Sinn Féiners had taken possession of the GPO [General Post Office] and several other public buildings. Rumours had begun to grow and reports began to fly. We made for town by the next tram and found we could only get as far as Amiens Street Station. We got off and walked up to [North] Earl Street. Crowds had gathered and they seemed to be getting nervous. Just as I arrived at the Pillar there was a crack of glass and the crowd rushed. At such a moment you don't know what is going to happen, so we stood against the wall. I then advanced when part of the crowd had gone by. There was a Dollymount tram at the corner of Earl Street. I suppose it was to act as a barricade. I got into O'Connell Street. It did look ghastly.

Two dead horses lay on the pavement. Not a sinner was in the middle of the street. Crowds were at the corners. Soldiers were over on the far side of the street taking cover behind railings etc trying to fire at somebody or something in the GPO. Suddenly shots rang out and there was a howl and screeching set up by the women. A priest stood near. I went over to him. "Shall I go

Postcard: Guarding North Earl Street

GPO, O'Connell Street

over", he said "and get the soldiers to withdraw. There is no use firing into the air like that. The people will suffer for it". "If you can see the officer", I said, "it would be the best thing possible". He went up along the crowd and crossed over, got up to the soldiers, and spoke to them. The soldiers walked away and went towards the Rotunda [Hospital].[4]

I was altogether puzzled. What had taken place? I wanted to find out the truth. I walked up a bit, but Harry wanted me to come back. I held out and he went back to get Johanna, who had remained in Earls Street. I met an old man at the corner and he told me he had been up at Kingsbridge [Railway Station] to meet some friends of his who were to be in Dublin at noon. No trains came in and there was a report, he said, that the train from Kilkenny had been derailed. What the exact truth of this point was I could never find out. There seems to have been some kind of hold up of trains by the Volunteers but the extent is not exactly known. Groups were already forming and the wildest reports were out. "The Volunteers had captured the Telephone Exchange. The Bank of Ireland was in their hands. The Lord Lieutenant was a prisoner in the Vice-Regal Lodge. The Volunteers had taken the Castle and were master of the Green [St Stephen's], Jacobs [factory], the [Phoenix] Park..."[5] You might go on for ever and never reach the end of the series of reports.

I got up to half way through O'Connell Street and saw a Volunteer on the roof of the GPO. He seemed to be anxious to settle something. As it turned out afterwards, he was setting up a flag pole on which he wanted to hoist the Republican flag. More Volunteers were at the windows or at least in the holes where the windows used to be, for all the glass was smashed and chairs, tables, and even mail-bags were piled up to afford protection for the men who wished to fire from these places. The hotels were all closed and the whole place seemed to have put on suddenly a besieged air. Policemen were standing in doorways afraid to stir out lest bullets might find them. I got up as far as Findlaters Place [off Upper O'Connell Street] and saw about 24 policemen standing there under cover. Certainly the bullets from the

catalogue.nli.ie

BERESFORD PLACE SHOWING LIBERTY HALL

> GPO could not find them there. I spoke to the Sergeant who did not know what had happened. All he was aware of was that bullets were flying about O'Connell Street and that it would not be safe for him and his men to be out there. I told him what I had heard. He seemed thunderstruck altogether.
>
> I passed on up to Parnell Street, and there I found the squadron of Lancers, who had beat such a hasty retreat from the Pillar and in doing so had left two of their horses dead in the street. There seemed to be almost fifty drawn up in front of the Rotunda Hospital. All were fully armed, rifles, lances, revolvers etc. The poor officer in charge did seem blue, and he looked as if he could wish to be any place else except where he was. He really did not know what to do.

Also for Monday, Delaney had brief, difficult-to-read notes indicating that he had visited other places and reported the comments of people he had met. Thus, he passed by Liberty Hall and found it quiet; spoke with Fr Curran, Archbishop Walsh's secretary, at Drumcondra; experienced looting at Earls Street; and at the GPO he witnessed Volunteers outside the gate with fixed bayonets, and 'Volunteers in the GPO talking to

...sday. Liberty Hall windows down perfectly quiet. I part with O.B. there & then go up Abbey st. but can't pass barricade made of, like crates sewer pipes benches etc. Go down [illegible] & up Sackville place where another barricade I get in by side of it & get into O'Connell st. People walking up and down. Shops looted. Mansfield's open at corner of Abbey st. & other shops. Barbed wire across from G.P.O. to tram pole & all the side ~~streets~~ blocked with barricades.

Pass up by G.P.O. Volunteers on Roof. inside fl[ag] hoisted Republican colours & green flag with words "Irish Republic". Earl st blocked Cathedral place looting. Man passing across [illegible] st. from Rotunda Hospital with flitch of bacon. I then passed up Britain st. & saw people barricading their shop windows. Th[en] I passed down Marlborough st. People running across with all kinds of loot. Then I went into Earl st. & saw shops looted

Stackeys. Reillys Cab-ordes. also Catholic Repository
Passed along & saw nothing till I came to Long Lane & saw
Soldiers guarding Lynch's Shop. Shots ringing out.
I got home & learned from Mother that ~~she~~ she saw early before
2 motor cars held up at Liberty hall & brought ~~under~~ under arch
also cab & horse also 2 motor lorries of Cauliflowers
which were attacked by mob till driven off by Citizen
Army. Whilst she was there, great cheering ~~owing~~ as a lorry
filled with ammunition stopped at Liberty hall cases
brought in. also at that morning at 7.30 she saw
at Annesley Bridge one motor car held up an old
gent. very angry but Volunteers controlled & drove down
side road. She sees Volunteers on roof of Manure
Coy's offices. Mr Donaldson comes back from Shipyard
& says Bridges are up & could not get into Ship yard
~~as Germans had landed~~ Soldiers on guard told by Soldiers
that Germans had landed. Dreadful heavy shooting
I go [illegible] D O.B. sees [illegible] lorry of Guinness on Annesley
Bridge. & motor van at Ranes. ~~[illegible]~~
not to pass over Bridge. Pass down Leinster Ave &
see O.B. who tells me he had stayed in by luck as

Two pages from John Delaney SJ's diary

people', and 'Volunteers marching up with a box with ginger-beer and sandwiches'. At the same time, there was 'a very jolly chap at the Pillar singing and shouting "Home Rule".' On a more urgent note, he commented that 'O'B' (Fr O'Brien from Milltown Park)[6] called on them at number 13 and told them of his giving absolution under fire. Later, Delaney briefly noted – 'fight between Volunteers and soldiers on Leinster Avenue. O'B crawling into on his stomach'. He reported that the nephew of Michael Davitt had been killed, and, referring to widespread rumours, he had heard that 'Kilkenny is in arms. There is Rising all over Ireland. Limerick is up. Cork up. Galway the only place that did not succeed'.

Tuesday, 25 April

Under this date, Delaney wrote at length.[7] The bitty nature of his entries convey the confusion of the time. He and O'B parted company at Liberty Hall, which was 'perfectly quiet'. Delaney then went up Abbey Street but could not pass further because of 'barricades made of crates, sewer pipes, benches etc'. He managed to get up to Sackville Place, where he met a further barricade. By the side of it, he managed to get to O'Connell Street, where 'people were walking up and down. Shops were looted'. But 'Mansfields [shoe shop] was open at the corner of Abbey Street, and other shops'. There was barbed wire near the GPO and 'all the side streets were blocked with barricades'. There were Volunteers on the roof of the GPO hoisting 'green flags with the words "Irish Republic".' He saw widespread looting at Catherine Place, Marlborough Street and Earls Street. 'A man passed across O'Connell Street from the Rotunda Hospital with flitches of bacon.' Not surprisingly, as Delaney passed up Britain Street he 'saw people barricading their shop windows'.

When he got to his mother's house, he learned from her that on the previous evening she saw 'two motor cars held up at Liberty Hall… and also a cab and a horse'. 'Two motor lorries of cauliflowers were attacked by a mob, but were driven off by the Citizen Army. While she was there, there was great cheering and up came a lorry filled with ammunition. It stopped at Liberty Hall and cases were brought in.' Delaney noted that the Volunteers were still firing down Leinster Avenue at soldiers on the railway. On the wider reports or rumours, he was told that transport ships were in the river; that a gun boat and torpedo destroyer had arrived,

A poster found amongst the belongings of John Delaney SJ of the Leaders of the Insurrection, May, 1916

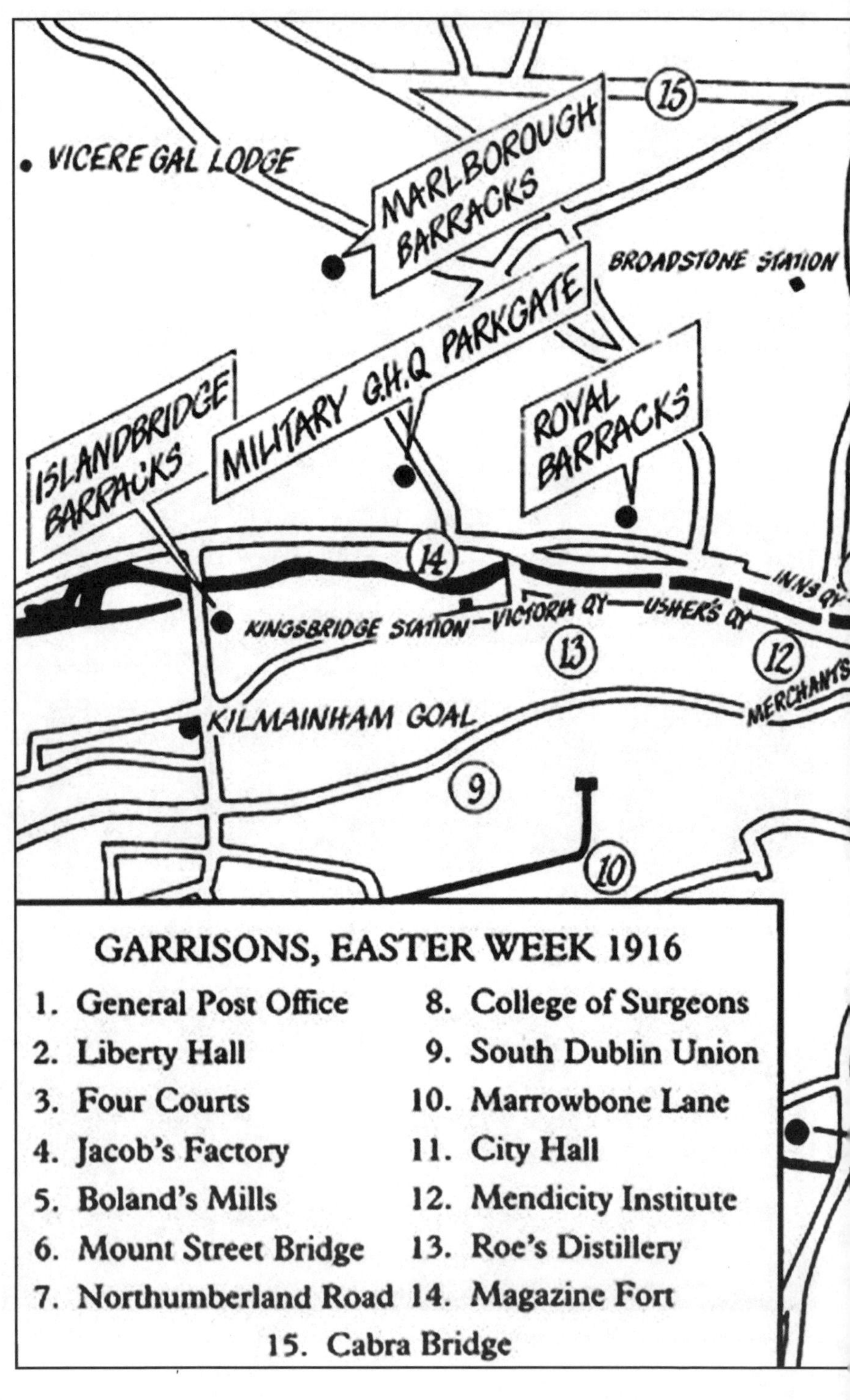
VICEREGAL LODGE
MARLBOROUGH BARRACKS
15
BROADSTONE STATION
MILITARY G.H.Q PARKGATE
ISLANDBRIDGE BARRACKS
ROYAL BARRACKS
14
INNS QY
KINGSBRIDGE STATION
VICTORIA QY
USHER'S QY
13
12
MERCHANTS
KILMAINHAM GOAL
9
10
GARRISONS, EASTER WEEK 1916
1. General Post Office
2. Liberty Hall
3. Four Courts
4. Jacob's Factory
5. Boland's Mills
6. Mount Street Bridge
7. Northumberland Road
8. College of Surgeons
9. South Dublin Union
10. Marrowbone Lane
11. City Hall
12. Mendicity Institute
13. Roe's Distillery
14. Magazine Fort
15. Cabra Bridge

OUNTJOY PRISON
N
NENHALL
RRACKS
PARNELL ST
SACKVILLE ST
AMIENS ST STATION
HENRY ST
1
2
CUSTOM HOUSE
ABBEY ST
WESTLAND ROW ST.
RIVER LIFFEY
PEARSE ST
NGTON QY
DAME ST
TRINITY COLLEGE
11
GRAFTON ST
NASSAU ST
5
GRAND CANAL ST
MOUNT ST
AUNGIER ST
4
8
CLANWILLIAM HOUSE
6
NORTHUMBERLAND RD.
ST STEPHEN'S GREEN
7
OURT ST STATION
BEGGARS BUSH
BARRACKS
VELLINGTON
RRACKS
PORTOBELLO
BARRACKS

and that troops had been landed at Kingstown (Dun Laoghaire). The hospitals were full, and the morgue was full of dead people. Feeling sceptical about so many reports, Delaney, passing down Amien Street, called into the morgue. When asked how many corpses were in the morgue, the official stated – four. 'One was a soldier, who was asphyxiated because he forgot to turn off the gas in his room; another was a sailor who fell off his boat into the river and was drowned; another, an old man who fell down stairs and broke his neck; and the fourth was as a result of an accident.'

'We passed on our way,' Delaney added, 'having exploded that bubble, and passed over by the Custom House, where all seemed quiet and peaceful.' But 'suddenly a voice rang out from the Custom House window: "If you pass this way again you will be shot". I [Delaney] looked to see where the voice was coming from and saw two officers sitting at the window which was raised a little.'

He continued:

> We passed quickly and got over Butt Bridge, where youngsters passed by with loot. Amongst others, [there was] a boy riding a huge elephant, which caused wonderful excitement as soon as it appeared on the City Quay side. All the women and children running and shouting with delight. We passed down along the quay, and as we got opposite the Custom House, very heavy firing started right behind us, as if it were up in the North Circular Road about Phibsborough. It continued and we passed down.

Checking on the stories he had heard, Delaney 'strained to see the transports and gunboats' but 'could see nothing'. 'I made enquiries and found that no boat had come in with troops nor was there any gunboat. Soldiers were doing sentry work in the different sheds but these had come from the different barracks. Another bubble burst. We passed down.' Forbes Street by the gasworks was quiet:

> Here Fr O'B and myself parted with Harry and continued up along the Grand Canal quay by the "Cats and Dogs" [public house]. Here everything was quiet. So quiet that I suspected something – especially as I passed under the railway bridge. It must have been suggestion, as this place proved to be one of the chief strongholds of the Volunteers.

catalogue.nli.ie

O'CONNELL STREET

A busy O'Connell Street with pedestrians and trams, a shelled GPO, and Nelson's Pillar

As we came out onto Grand Canal Street we saw about seven Volunteers get possession of the house on the right hand side of the street. Boland's [Mills] on the left was already fortified with sandbags etc. The canal bridge was blocked by bread vans. There we were told that the Volunteers occupied the houses all along the canal up to Leeson Street, and were holding the Protestant school and parochial hall in Northumberland Road. The telephone and electrical lines were cut on this bridge and in the ground. We passed on and continued our journey, but we noticed military-looking men in mufti on bikes examining all the places along.

We got back to Milltown and heard the following: that there had been a terrible fight on Portobello Bridge . . ., that hard fights had taken place at the South Dublin Union, [and] Leonard's Corner on Circular Road, that several arrests had been made, amongst others Sheehy Skeffington, editor of the *Eye Opener* etc, that transports had arrived and had been seen.

Delaney was able to contradict this last, but was told that the transports had moved to Kingstown (Dun Laoghaire). As he had not visited Kingstown, he could not say if this were true or not. Among other pronouncements, it was announced that Guinness[8] and the Four Courts were in the hands of the Volunteers.

Wednesday, 26 April

Delaney's entry for the day begins: 'I go towards Portobello and meet Mrs Redmond, who tells us that her brother, Mr. Kavanagh, insurance agent of Liberty Hall, was killed on the steps of that house the day before.' Delaney interrupted his narrative at this point to mention what he termed 'wild reports':

> Fr McCann[9] states that Liberty Hall was blown to bits. A messenger coming with supplies reported that Liberty Hall and the South Dublin Union were in bits, he had seen this with his own eyes. Fr McCann's brother is reported as saying that 5,000 troops had landed that morning and were marching on Dublin, and that artillery had gone out to the hills.

Delaney set out to check the veracity of these and other reports. He at least found out that there was no evidence of artillery being posted on the hills, and as to military success by the troops at Portobello, he found 'the military under cover behind the garden wall opposite Rathmines Church' and that, just before he arrived, a soldier who had tried to cross Portobello Bridge was shot dead. While Delaney was there, 'shots ring out to prove that Volunteers still hold up the army'.

On Wednesday morning, setting out from Milltown Park, Delaney met a young fellow who told him he was a Volunteer, that his rifle, uniform and equipment were in his house on Rathmines Road. He left the house that morning. His wife remained behind. Now he hears that his house has been searched. He asks Delaney what is he to do? If he returns home, a soldier may be awaiting him. If he does not go home, he may be arrested. He cannot go to his brother's house 'as he is not fighting', and his friend's house on Burgh Quay was cut off and surrounded. Nothing if not resourceful, Delaney advised him 'to send a girl to his wife to know definitely if the house had been searched. If not, go home and hide rifle and uniform under the floor boards under the table. If the house had

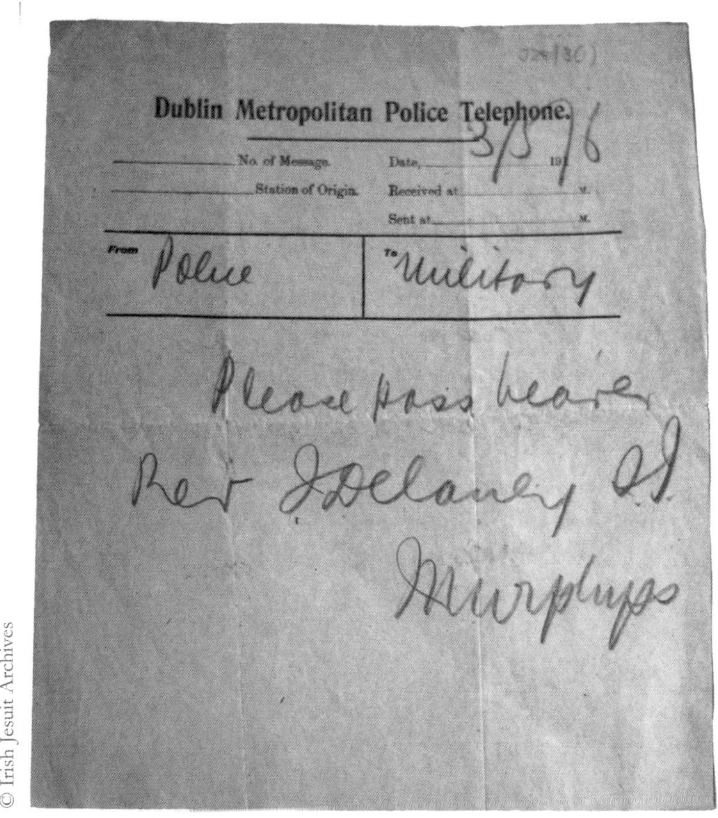

Dublin Metropolitan Police Telephone.

No. of Message — Date, 3/5/16

Station of Origin — Received at ____ M.

Sent at ____ M.

From Police — To Military

Please pass bearer

Rev J Delaney SJ

Murphy

JOHN DELANEY'S DAY PASS

Dated 3 May 1916, John Delaney SJ had learned that to move freely around Dublin city relied on obtaining a Pass from the police to inform the military to grant the bearer access

been searched, 'find out if anything had been found. If not, return. If anything had been found, to know exactly what and then act accordingly.' Delaney continued:

> We pass along the canal and meet Br Naughton on Charleville Bridge, who tells us that he had been across town and had been helped across two barricades by the Volunteers, that all were still holding to the places they had already captured. He told the Volunteers that the military had landed and were advancing against them. "Let them come", was the reply. "We are ready for them"… We passed over the road and down along the canal towards Leeson Street Bridge on which there was a single soldier

in full kit. Some barge men told us that the military had fired on them that morning and had ordered them to leave their boats. When we came to Leeson Street Bridge we found a company of soldiers of the Notts & Derby regiment resting on the steps of the houses. The officers were out on the road examining maps of the city and wearing rather puzzled looks. They were being informed of all necessary details by men in mufti who were to be seeing [sic] going hither and thither on bikes.

We passed down by the soldiers to Leeson Street Church. The Tommies looked very tired and weary, as they had marched in from Kingstown under a broiling sun along the dusty roads. They were eating biscuits, drinking tea, and smoking cigarettes, which had been given them by the people, especially the Protestants, who now wore peaceful looking countenances as the soldiers had freed them from the Catholics and this awful Romish plot, as they said. We waited at the church and up came the Notts & Derby regiment[10] led by officers who did not know, it seemed, where they were. As they were looking at their maps, one young fellow shouted to the crowd – "Where is the bridge? We have to advance to the bridge", and the bridge was only some yards in front of him.

The advance party then advanced very slowly across the bridge; when suddenly one solitary shot rang out. All looked towards the house whence it was supposed to have come, but nothing followed. All the troops advanced, following the ordinary military tactics: scout, advance party, then the main body, and all cross the bridge and pass along the Adelaide Road. The crowds at Leeson Street Church expected the Volunteers to oppose the march of the soldiers, as it was reported that the houses all round the bridge and down Leeson Street were occupied by the Volunteers. One old gentleman said to me – "Now it will be all over and compulsion [conscription] will be passed and enforced in Ireland". "Do you really thinks so?" I asked. "Yes", he said. "Do you really think", I asked him, "that the Government will give rifles into the hands of these men again?" "Well, I didn't think of that", came the reply.

Delaney, as indicated earlier, did not escape the widespread view among Catholics that identified Protestants with a condescending ascendancy class more English than the English. This was evident in his succeeding narrative:

'We passed down Waterloo Place and saw the Protestants all out on their door steps waving hands to the soldiers; and some old dames of the grey hair and spectacles type, with the real sourface displayed to perfection, ran over and offered two oranges to 200 men.' Delaney's companion, Padraig, 'was furious'.

> The soldiers were still advancing from Donnybrook, where it is reported they met with a very unwelcome reception. We passed down Eglinton Place and down the Wellington Road, where people seemed somewhat nervous. As we came to Clyde Road, we got sight of the first house being surrounded by the soldiers. They were crouching all along the walls. Some had crossed into the gardens, when there was a shout from the officer – "Let no man pass". Suddenly, two young girls rushed out of the laneway shrieking, and the soldiers, who were crouching under the wall, got up to run after them with fixed bayonets.
>
> In two minutes, out from the laneway marched a guard of soldiers with fixed bayonets guarding 6 men and one boy, who were all marched off. They were not Volunteers as it turned out but were found in the stables of the houses and were arrested as suspects. The Protestants at the corners of the roads were delighted and were giving all the information possible to the soldiers. We then advanced to the Pembroke Road, where we got under cover of the wall and had a view of Ballsbridge. The soldiers were lying on their stomachs, in open formation right across the road, down beyond the Town Hall and the Dublin Society show grounds. The soldiers had surrounded this corner house and were endeavouring to penetrate it when, out from Hammersmith Works, rang rifle shots and all, including the soldiers, crouched under cover of the wall. The poor old Protestant minister, who had been giving all the information, could hardly bend over and I was afraid every moment to see him fall. But the Volunteers were only after the military. We left this danger zone and watched matters at a distance, but finding it near dinner time

we progressed in the direction of Milltown Park.

At the corner of the Clyde Road, we met a real sourface type of Protestant carrying a basket with 7 cups in one hand and a large jug of tea in the other. She wished to go down to the house where the soldiers were. I warned her that there was firing going on. She ... got under cover. I left her to her own sweet will.

At Milltown I heard that the firing of the Volunteers was deadly, and that several of the soldiers had been picked off while advancing in skirmishing order. An English Jesuit scholastic, who had been down to see the troops come in, wished to speak to some of the soldiers but when he saw the crowd of Protestants at the end of Ailsbury Road and saw the kind they were – all of the real sourface disposition and the grey hair-and-spectacle type clapping hands and saying to one another "Clap, clap, clap for the soldiers. Now we are saved" – he would not speak to any of the soldiers lest he might mix with such a crowd. "I understood for the first time in my life", he said, "what loyalty in Ireland means, and I recognised that to sing 'God Save the King' in Dublin meant to sing 'To Hell with the Pope'". He came back dejected... Another English scholastic [Mr. Wilson] stated that the [army] chaplain told him that the men got word on Monday night and left next morning for France or Mesopotamia as they thought. It was only when they got to Liverpool that they heard for the first time that they were going instead to Dublin to quell a riot, as they were told. They were to find out for themselves that the *riot* was rather serious and was to deprive them of a number of their men.

After dinner I left for Ballsbridge, where the fight was still going on. The soldiers were still on the ground and were advancing slowly, always observing the open formation and lying on their stomachs. There was a big crowd around the Town Hall, and some members of the [army] staff were to be seen with their *aides de camp*.

Suddenly, at the end of Pembroke Road appeared a number of prisoners surrounded by a cordon of soldiers with fixed bayonets, which were pointed at the prisoners and not, as is usual, on the soldiers' shoulders. The soldiers who were lying on the road stood up and allowed the prisoners to pass. As they passed I could count them. They were eleven, amongst them being two women, one of whom was rather fashionably dressed. There was one like a DMP [Dublin Metropolitan Policeman], 2 or 3 were rather poorly dressed, and in the last line were two rather old men with white hair but who seemed to be in quite good humour as they were smoking, talking and laughing as they marched by. They were all brought into the Town Hall enclosure and there, in the front of the Hall in the presence of the whole crowd, they were searched by an officer. Rifles were pointed at them the whole time by soldiers placed around. When the searching was over, they were all marched out of the enclosure and followed the main body of the soldiers, who had been ordered to advance as the officers thought all was over.

There was one man, with no hat on and looking very determined, under a very special guard. All advanced up along the Pembroke Road, soldiers, prisoners, carts, wagons. Suddenly, all came to a halt at the entrance of Northumberland Road, and the carts, prisoners, and a number of the soldiers were sent back to the Town Hall. Evidently, the soldiers had been led into a trap and the [military] staff had to rearrange their plans. The staff had forgotten one thing – that the Volunteers were soldiers also, and had done a little "tactics" during their spare time.

Thursday, 27 April – Friday 28 April

Thursday morning brought more reports:[11] Jacobs burned down, different buildings shelled. Acting, however, on the principle not to take those [reports] without proof, I go into town with Fr O'Brien. We pass down Leeson Street, where everything is perfectly quiet. The Red Cross flags were flying from the private hospital of St Vincent's. Several houses looked very suspicious as the blinds were drawn. Those opposite our houses in [35 & 36] Leeson Street were reported to be occupied by Volunteers. We arrived at the Green where we saw things as they were since Monday. The gates were locked. The trams, cars, carts were drawn up as they were the first day.

A number of medical students were on the steps of St Vincent's

> Hospital talking to Fr Tom Finlay.[12] All seemed to be in great spirits and were chatting about the state of Dublin.' As regards St Vincent's Hospital, 'wild rumours had gone abroad to the effect that medical aid, in the shape of nurses and doctors, had been asked for. Mrs Carew,[13] the Revd Mother of the hospital, had refused. So people said. Fr John Hannon[14] went into the hospital and asked the Revd Mother if this is the true story.' She explained that 'St Vincent's Hospital was rung up by Countess Markievicz and medical aid was asked for. As the countess was speaking, the military, who were in possession of the [Telephone] Exchange, cut off the countess. She was in the College of Surgeons, which was held by the Volunteers. St Vincent's was told that anybody daring to go over to the Volunteers would be shot. Mrs Carew announced this and a young fellow named McNamara, a medical student, offered to go across to the College of Surgeons.
>
> He was received at the door of the college by an armed guard. He told the officer in charge that he was a medical student, that he was not a Sinn Féiner and did not sympathise with them, and was, in fact, going to join the army as soon as he was qualified. "Very well", replied the Volunteer officer, "I shall treat you, and see that you are treated, as a medical man".

There was one wounded person, a young girl who was wounded in the arm and the thigh. The student dressed the wounds and left. He was 'highly delighted with all he saw in the Volunteers' quarters. He spoke very highly of them and said that he found only one wounded there'. This 'dispelled the rumours that many wounded lay there'. Delaney heard the above account from Fr Hannon, who had spoken with the young medical student when he returned to the hospital.

Delaney continued his narrative: 'I passed by, therefore, St Vincent's Hospital and just as I came to Dominican Hall, 2 or 3 doors down from Hume Street, a rifle shot rang out.' He thought it was from the Shelbourne Hotel. But some said it was from the College of Surgeons, but, in his view, it was too near for that. He continued:

> We turned down Hume Street and found a number of old ladies at the doors pointing to places where the bullets were supposed to have hit. We passed on and down Merrion Square 'till we came to Nassau Street. Up along Mount Street there was

catalogue.nli.ie

TROOPS INSPECTING A CAR ON MOUNT STREET BRIDGE, 1916

heavy fighting and grenades were being freely used. We passed on down along Westland Row, where we saw some shops that had been looted. The railway station was barricaded but quite silent. Crowds had gathered at the corner of Brunswick Street [now Pearse Street][15] and were looking towards Boland's Mills where there was very heavy firing, and also up towards the Queen's Theatre where the military had taken up their positions.

We passed on and tried to get down to the quay by some of the back streets, when suddenly there was a rush of women calling out for a priest. Man shot. We ran whither we were directed, and then Fr O'Brien and myself had all the blessing of heaven called down on us by the poor women, who greeted us with the following: "Oh God bless the priests. Sure they are always there when you want them. Oh what would we do only for our holy priests. May the Blessed Mother guard and protect them". We got up to the man. He was badly wounded in the upper leg. Fr O'Brien went up to him and found he was a Protestant. "Get me an ambulance if you can, Father", said the poor man. So Fr O'Brien turned away to fetch the ambulance, and some asked – "Will he not go to confession, Father?" "Oh, he is a Protestant", replied Fr O'Brien. And then, with all the simplicity possible, said a young fellow: "But Father could you not make him turn before he dies". The faith of these poor people is really wonderful. We went then to fetch the ambulance but found all the road barred by the military, who demanded a military pass. I told them I was going for the ambulance, so they allowed me to pass up to Tara Street. I went into the station and found that all the ambulances were out gathering in the wounded. I turned back and found one coming up the road from Westland Row. Fr McCann SJ was in front with the driver. He was going over to the Custom House where a wounded Catholic was looking for a priest. We sent the stretcher-bearers down for the poor man. When they got there, they found him in a hand cart being wheeled along by a couple of men to Jervis Street [Hospital].

We had no military passes, so we had to come back... We began to retrace our steps 'till we came to Merrion Square. At Hollis Street corner we witnessed the Mount Street battle going on. The firing was terrific. Hand grenades were being hurled at the houses in which the Volunteers were. The din was dreadful and the explosions of the grenades were awful. But the soldiers could not advance. Three times the soldiers advanced to take the house after all this bombing and three times were they met with the most deadly rifle fire from the Volunteer rifles, and three times the soldiers ran away and down the Beggars Bush Road. The officers rallied the men again, and with grenades they burned the houses and thus drove the Volunteers on to the roofs of the houses in Mount Street. Whilst we were at Hollis Street corner, a shot rang out from the top of the house. The shot proved to be from the military, who had got on to the top of these houses in order to counter the retreat of the Volunteers.

We moved off once more from the danger zone and went up Baggot Street. Just at the convent [of the Mercy Sisters] we met Fr Wall, curate of Haddington Road Catholic Church. He gave us an account of the seizure of the Catholic Church by the military and of the fight round about. He told us of the death of Lieutenant Hawkin, who was shot by the Volunteers. He was

> carried into a neighbouring house, asked for a priest, who went out under fire, got to the Lieutenant, gave him the last sacraments and, while by his side, young Hawkin breathed his last. The priest then endeavoured to get back but was held up by the military, who thought he was a Volunteer in disguise. As we parted with Fr Wall, the fight was still going on. Ambulances were flying about in all directions. Two were drawn up in front of the City of Dublin Hospital in Baggot Street.

At this point, Delaney broke off to tell of 'a great report about Bishop Donnelly' which was 'told by a Protestant minister'. Delaney reports:

> I give it for what it is worth, as I did not see Bishop Donnelly to ask him. It seems that when the fight on Haddington Road was at its height and several wounded lay on the road, the bishop walked out into the middle of the road holding up his hands and shouting at the top of his voice – "I shall remain here 'till all the wounded are removed". The firing ceased once the bishop went out. The Red Cross came out, carried off the wounded, and then when all had been removed the bishop withdrew and the firing restarted. Such is the story told by the Protestant minister.

Resuming his narrative from Baggot Street, Delaney reported that 'hearing the rumble of military wagons', he 'looked up and saw huge carts, field kitchens etc being brought across Leeson Street Bridge'.

> I went along Mespil Road, to see them pass. We got up to the bridge to see the last of the field kitchens pass across the bridge and proceed up along the Adelaide Road. They seemed to fear Leeson Street yet and would not dare appear near the Green, still a stronghold of the Volunteers. The North Staffordshire Regiment was drawn up in Upper Leeson Street. A large naval gun was mounted on a lorry, which was in charge of a detachment of the naval brigade. The officers were very young and inexperienced looking. Suddenly despatch raiders came up and orders were given to return to Ballsbridge. The orders rang out, but the poor Tommies seemed very raw indeed as they had to order "Number Off" twice and "Form Fours" three times before they did it properly. Off they marched then, leaving a crowd of

> open-mouthed wonderers. "Where are they going?" "What is the matter now?" were the usual questions, and nobody could answer, not even the officers.
>
> A priest came up and told us that 40 pieces of artillery had gone up Adelaide Road. He saw them himself, he said. They were in reality the field kitchens that I had seen passing. The chimneys were down and at a distance they did look like guns. That is how reports grow! I met Fr Jack Byrne,[16] who told us that there was a great rumour that Sheehy Skeffington[17] was shot. One thing was certain that he was a prisoner in Porto Bello [sic] Barracks, but as to the death it was only a rumour or there was no official confirmation. He tells us of a sad but beautiful, even heroic, case. "I said Mass", he said, "for an Irish Volunteer this morning. The wife brought me 5 shillings (5/-) and asked to have the Mass this morning. Her husband had been out fighting from the first day, had been wounded in two places, [and] had been taken to Stephen's Hospital in his uniform. A young doctor dressed the wounds, having extracted two bullets, and gave him a suit of his to go home. The young Volunteer went to see his wife, and left in the early hours of the morning to go back to the GPO to fight it out." A magnificent example of bravery!

By this it was evident where John Delaney's sympathies lay. He continued:

> We got back to Ranelagh, where we saw some of the grandest ladies and gents carrying home their shopping – cabbages, bread, meat. It was a strange sight to see all of all classes thus doing their bit. We came across a proclamation of martial law ordering us to be in by 7.30pm and to keep away from the areas where military operations were being carried on. This was another proof of the stern reality that was on us.
>
> After dinner, I went off towards Rathmines and found the military around about Ranelagh. They were examining the district and searching the houses along Oakley Road, where Pearse's sisters live as also McDonagh's wife.[18] We were allowed to pass and got out on the Rathmines Road and turned our steps towards Portobello Barracks. The road was deserted; and all around the

PADRAIG PEARSE

Right: A piece of the cloth off the coat P Pearse wore when he was shot. Below: The envelope in which the piece of cloth was received and kept by John Delaney SJ

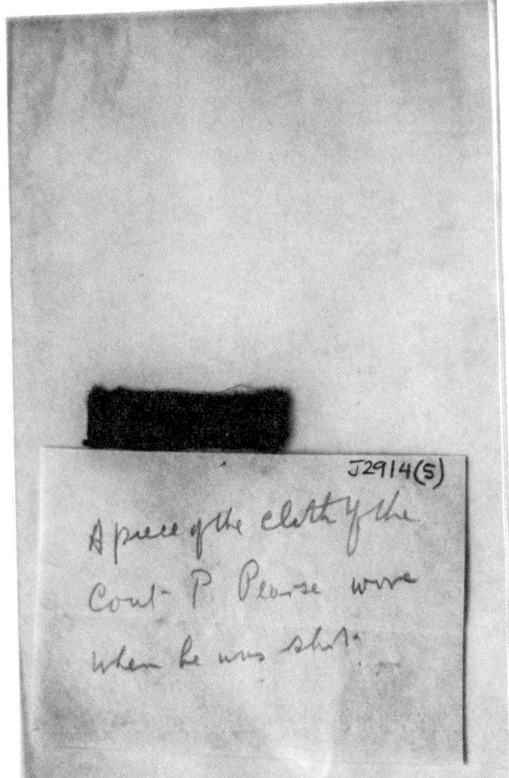

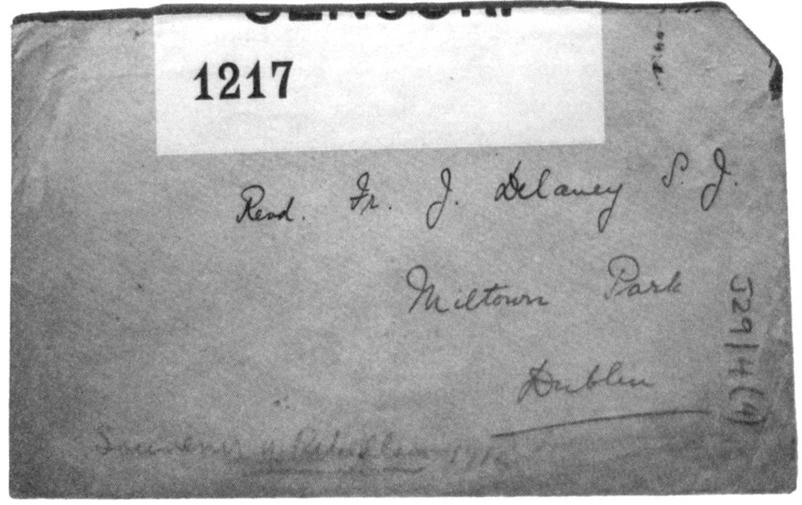

barracks, grounds, houses, gardens were guarded by soldiers and a few members of the RIC [Royal Irish Constabulary]. Firing was still going on at the bridge over the canal. Wild reports were floating round about men being shot by the soldiers in the middle of the street. One was that the soldiers had surrounded a house and had succeeded in getting one Volunteer. This man was brought out and asked to surrender. He is supposed to have said – "I never surrender to a Sassan [ach]", and was shot immediately. Another was that a young boy was brought out and was ordered to kneel down in the middle of Charlemont Street and was shot dead by the soldiers. These were reports. Whether they are true or not I don't know. Personally, I don't believe them.

As we stood in front of the barrack's gate, I saw a young Volunteer marched up along the road by an armed guard. The Volunteer's head was bandaged up. A few Protestant-looking individuals of the real sourface type gathered and stood near me. One especially took my fancy. He stood near me and said aloud, but for my benefit, as the prisoner passed us – "He won't be alive this time tomorrow evening". I said nothing. "He'll be shot and be a dead man by this time tomorrow evening", he continued, all of course for my benefit. I could not resist. So I said – "Oh, indeed". "Yes", he continued, "We'll shoot them all down". "But you didn't shoot them in South Africa", I said. "De Wet and company are still alive. You didn't shoot them". "No", he said, "but we'll shoot them [the Volunteers]". "Oh", I said, "are you a German?" "No", he replied, "I'm not". "I thought you were from the policy you advocate of shooting down people. Wasn't the essence of all the Recruiting Posters in Ireland to ask for men to put down this kind of militarism of shooting down people?" "Yes", he said, "but didn't you know it was all hypocrisy on our part". "Then you are a hypocrite", I said. "You don't mean what you say. Good evening". And thus I left him to his fate, boiling all over for he had led himself into the trap in which I caught him so nicely. The few ladies standing round looked at him and smiled at me as I walked away and left him to his thoughts.

TROOPS BEING MARCHED TO BARRACKS, 1916

Self-satisfied with his inconsequential victory, Delaney passed down by a side street, where he met 'a great sympathiser of the Volunteers'. 'Is there any news?', Delaney queried:

> "Ain't they fighting bravely" [said the sympathiser]. The "Boys", as they endearingly called the Volunteers, were described as "giving it hot to the military and it wasn't all over with them yet. Heavy fighting was still going on at Dolphin's Barn, up at the South Dublin Union, down at Ringsend, and all over the city. Liquid fire had been used by the military on the Volunteers defending the Post Office". I did not like to believe this last statement, but there seems to be something in it. For three girls, who had been there nursing the wounded, confirmed it. You may take it for what it is worth.
>
> We passed on and came out on Ranelagh Road and met a young man, a prominent architect of the city, who is a National Volunteer,[19] a follower of John Redmond. He told us that all the places in town were still holding out, that he had been through town in the early part of the day, that the firing along the quays was very violent, and that he himself had nearly been potted several times, especially on the Metal Bridge, by soldiers who were

on top of the Telephone Exchange in Crown Alley. All in town, by the way, expressed their surprise that the Volunteers did not seize the Telephone Exchange. A couple of days ago, however, I learned from one man that the reason was that the Germans had planned the whole *coup*, and thinking that the Telephone Exchange was in the GPO, as it is always on the Continent, that once the GPO was in their hands by that very fact they had the Telephone Exchange. That is only by the way… Well, the young architect told us that there had been a deputation to the Lord Mayor to ask him to intervene and try to get the Volunteers to come to some kind of terms with the military, but that he said it would serve them right to be all wiped out. Seeing no chance there, the deputation proceeded to Nathan, the Under Secretary, who received them very well and said he would do all he could with the Lord Lieutenant,[20] but the answer of the latter was – "The military have taken the whole affair in hand. I cannot intervene".

The deputation was, naturally enough, angered at this, and just at this point as he was talking to us, out boomed a couple of shells again, and away rattled the machine guns. It was awful to listen to. We bid him good evening, and hurried home as it was nearing 7.30pm the hour prescribed by martial law. We met several hurrying home to be indoors by the appointed hour. We smiled at one another for we all understood one another's motive of haste. As we wended our way to Milltown we could see a big glow in the sky over the city. The fires had broken out. The bombs were doing their work. The rattle of the machine guns continued; and though we felt at such a distance yet the feeling of horror was beginning to spread. That evening we heard that several places in Ireland had risen in sympathy with Dublin, and that there was fear of the rebellion spreading to the west.

From the top of the roof of the house [at Milltown] we could see the fires – huge fires they were with flames, which seemed mountain high, leaping to the sky. And right through the whole thing boomed the guns and the never ending rattle of the machine gun with the continual reply of the Volunteers' rifle shot. Ypres, Louvain, Rheims, were before our mind's eye in a moment

"In reality, it was O'Connell Street that was in flames."

> and we thought – *war had come to us at last. Dublin was in flames. The roar of guns was in our ears, at our very door, and men were falling. Men were dying not on the fields of France or in the trenches of Flanders, but on the streets of Dublin.* It was really dreadful; too dreadful to look at, too dreadful to hear, too dreadful to think of... We went down to prayers. I could not help thinking of the poor fellows dying not so far from us amid the shot and shell whilst we repeated in our little chapel "*Ora pro nobis*".
>
> Speculation was rife as to the location of the fires. Some thought the GPO, others, Jacob's biscuit factory in Peter's Row off Aungier Street, others again, Trinity College, whilst more asserted that it was a distillery as the flames were too high for ordinary houses.

Delaney added at this point that:

> In reality, it was O'Connell Street that was in flames. The military were burning the Volunteers out. The first fire started in Lawrence's shops and then spread all around that block so that the houses on O'Connell Street were burned down.
>
> Next morning came in reports of the whereabouts of the fire,

but the reports were wild. We got some English papers and saw the first of the picture papers with some photographs of Volunteers and those engaged in the Rising. We hear about the rising in Wexford and over in Galway. Reports are wild and nobody can confirm them. After lunch, I go over to [the Jesuit community at] Rathfarnham [Castle] and hear that the soldiers are gone up to the hills to round up the Volunteers, who were supposed either to have escaped from town or to be coming from Wicklow or Wexford. But there seems to be no real eye witness. As we were in the castle, a *char-á-banc* full of soldiers flew by up to the hills. Whither exactly they were going and where were the Volunteers, nobody seems to know ...

As we were returning from the castle, the machine guns were rattling away. On the [River] Dodder's bank we met two scholastics, who were returning from Ringsend. They contradicted the report that Boland's Mills and the places round about held by the Volunteers had fallen. They said that the district was being shelled and the firing was very heavy, but the republican flag was still flying and there was no sign of surrender. Thus, no place had given up to the present, and thus all places were still flying the flag except Liberty Hall, which had been shelled from the river ...

That evening I went down by Ballsbridge, and all along the Dodder the firing was very heavy. We got as far as London Bridge Road, along which there wasn't a sign of life because the Volunteers held the railway bridge and swept both sides, [including] up by Beggars Bush Barracks so that the soldiers could not leave the barracks. The ambulance was the only thing I could see. The most peculiar thing about it was that the day before they [the Volunteers] had been all driven out of that district, and this evening they are all back again commanding the entrance to the barracks so that no military could go in or out. As we stood at the bridge, shells rang out and we were ordered away. We retired and turned our steps homeward. As we were just leaving the bridge, out rang a volley and the machine guns started their horrid rattling. The grenade explosions were awful and the idea that rose uppermost in my mind was – How can men live through it all? And yet they seemed to live through it all. In several places when the military advanced to take the place by a rush, they entered and found nobody. The [military] staff had forgotten one essential point, i.e. that the Volunteers had studied military tactics and knew the weak points.

On this road [Northumberland Road] the Volunteers proved it. The military sent up this scout who came back and reported "all calm". The advance party was then sent along and they passed along as well. Then came the main body, crawling on their hands, advancing a few yards at a time, then lying quietly for a time. The main body had advanced half way up the road when, suddenly, out rang rifle shots and several of the soldiers rolled over killed or wounded badly. The firing continued and the soldiers fell like flies. The officer fixed one house and riddled it. The Volunteers answered with the usual result, for the soldiers had absolutely no cover. The firing from this house died away and the officer, thinking that the Volunteers had been killed or wounded or that their ammunition had given out, encircled the building and advanced very cautiously. Gradually they got up to the house and were just going to charge when, suddenly, the whole house seemed to blaze, windows, doors and roof, and the soldiers fell again. The fight lasted in this manner the whole evening and throughout the whole night. Rifle grenades were used by the military with very little success.

I had to return to Milltown. Next morning, when we got down to the same place, the firing was still as heavy, in fact heavier, than the preceding evening. Fr McCann, from Milltown Park, had been out the whole evening and throughout the whole night on ambulance work. He picked up, in company with nurses and RAMC [Royal Army Medical Corps] men, the wounded and left the dead on the road. He brought 68 wounded into Sir Patrick Dunn's Hospital and 60 into the City of Dublin Hospital in Baggot Street.

As the Northumberland Road fight was proceeding, I went down Lansdowne Road where a company of soldiers were told off to search all the houses. The search was carried out as stupidly as the Northumberland Road had been attacked. A sentry was placed at the hall door. Four or five soldiers entered the house and examined all the rooms in a rather superficial way. In a few moments they came out and passed on to the next house, where the same manoeuvre was gone through with the like success. Not a single Volunteer was found, as if they were going to remain in the house 'till the soldiers came in. One house next the railway had been occupied by the Volunteers, as also Lansdowne Road station, but both had been evacuated that morning, making sure beforehand to tear up the rails, cut all the wires, and take anything away that was valuable. A few rifles etc were found in this house, which, by the way, belongs to Judge Johnson.[21] The poor officer was delighted to be able to bring something back to his superior officer.

The Protestants were delighted and offered cigars to the officer and cigarettes to the men. There were three or four men looking on at the soldiers falling in to march back. Suddenly, one of the Protestants went over to the officer and whispered something to him. An order rang out and one of the onlookers, a young man about 20 years old, was surrounded with bayonets. The officer questioned him and then called me over. "Would you know an Irishman", he asked. "Certainly", I said. "Is that young man there an Irishman?" "I think so, for I think he lives about this place as I saw him before, but I shall speak to him and I shall find out very quickly".

"But doesn't he look very pale", said the officer. "Yes, but you know there are pale Irishmen as well as rubicund sons of the soil. What is your name?" I asked the young fellow. "Pa-a-trick Tr a cey", drawled out the young fellow. "Oh", said I to the officer, "there is no doubt. It is a pure Dublin accent". "Can you assure me it is a Dublin accent?" "Certainly", I replied. "Well what are you doing about here?" said the officer to the young fellow. "Nawthing", said the young fellow. "You see", said the officer, turning to me, "He says 'nos-sings'. He is a German." "Oh, nonsense", I said. "There is not even a shadow of 'nos-sings'. It is a pure 'nawthing', pure Dublin accent." "Well can you guarantee that?" "Certainly", I said. "There is no doubt about it." So the young fellow was liberated, and I was glad to have been on the spot and thus liberated the young fellow from the stupidity of the young officer.

We passed along. Just as soon as I left the officer, out from the houses they had searched rang out rifle shots. You should have seen the officer's face, and I thought it better and safer for me to get out of the road. I passed up by Ballsbridge again and found the soldiers keeping back the crowd. Suddenly, shots rang out from the houses and the poor soldiers fled for cover, thinking it better to be behind the stone walls of the River Dodder than in the open road inviting Volunteer shots. The rearguard up near Northumberland Road felt quite happy to be away from all the fray, when suddenly a shot rang out of a house that had been searched and one of the soldiers rolled over. The military was simply bewildered. They did not know what to do. They thought it better to wait till darkness gave them some cover.

I returned to Milltown Park and found some eye-witnesses of the fight which had taken place in Haddington Road. The officer had been very brave. He stood in the middle of the road issuing orders to his men and bullets showering round him. The men were falling and he seemed to have a charmed life. I don't know whether he escaped or not. The Haddington Road fight had a tragic and sad side. Fr Wall, the curate, told me personally what follows.

Bishop Donnelly had ordered all the churches in the danger zone to be closed at mid-day. The day the military arrived, a special detachment was sent from Kingstown, with a magistrate of the place at their head, to occupy the Catholic Church on Haddington Road. They appeared before the gates at 2.00pm and naturally found them closed. They rang. The sacristan appeared. "Open the gates", the officer shouted. "Very well", replied the sacristan, "I shall go and get permission from the Bishop". "Open immediately or you are a dead man", replied the officer, and suddenly all the rifles were levelled at the sacristan. The gates swung open. "Now show us the way to the tower". "I cannot do that without his Lordship's permission", said the sacristan. "Lead on", and once more the bayonets were pointed at him. The poor sacristan marched through the church with the soldiers following him with fixed bayonets pointed at him. When they arrived at the door of the tower, they ordered the sacristan to stand by and the soldiers mounted the tower. They settled themselves in the openings and, just as they were all settled, the Volunteer rifle shots rang out and all the soldiers in the tower fell. Served them right.

Fr Wall went to the officer, who was in the sacristy and in a very bad way. He saw he had made a very bad mistake. "Why on earth did you send up your men into such an open tower? Did you not know that you were sending them to certain death?" "Oh", replied the officer, "I never knew that they were going to reply." Another example of the stupidity of the military throughout this whole business.

The firing continued and was very heavy in several of the districts. The South Circular Road seemed to be the scene of a very hard fought fight. Ringsend was also very hot. The wildest rumours were afloat. Verdun had fallen. France had made peace. The Germans had landed in England. The Germans had landed on the south coast of Ireland. One British transport had been sunk. Air raids on English coast towns. Kut had fallen. Kut had been relieved.[22] In fact, everything imaginable was reported. With such reports flying all round, I returned to dream amid the shot and shell and sleep the sleep of the just.

It was strange. All was strange. The whole country was strange. "It is the strangest country I've ever been in",[23] said a colonel on the Northumberland Road. "There you are. Men, women and even children, will lean out of your windows, will come to your hall doors, will stand at your garden gates looking on quite placidly at a pitched battle being fought out in the street before your house. I can't make these Irish out at all".

When we returned to Ballsbridge there was excitement. More troops had arrived and in their company they had their field kitchens. Crowds had gathered and were gathering. The Protestants were offering the soldiers tea, cake, cigarettes and other creature comforts. The officers looked young and inexperienced. The "subs" [subalterns][24] looked a finer type than their superiors. I spoke to one poor soldier who was a Catholic. "I haven't had a wink of sleep since Monday. I've been on the move ever since." And he looked tired, I must say, and [he] was doubly delighted when he was able to take off his pack and stretch his weary limbs on the grassy plot in front of the Royal Dublin Society's buildings at Ballsbridge.

When the soldiers got their packs off and were inside the railings, they became more communicative. One walked over to a sentry who was standing quite close to me. "How are things going on", he asked the sentry. "They are picking off our men in a dreadful way", the sentry replied. "Our fellows went up. Fortunately, I was left here on sentry duty. I'm afraid I shan't see a good number of them again." It was perfectly true. The Volunteers were picking off a great number, not merely on the South side but all round Dublin. We passed [for] home, and left the Tommies to their thoughts and imaginations.

The sky over the city was quite red, and we could see that more fires had broken out. Firing towards the centre of the city was very heavy. It did seem dreadful. That evening I watched the fires of the city from the roof of the house. Flames rose very high, and all the pictures of Ypres were then pronounced to be quite real. It really looked awful to see such flames and volumes of thick smoke ascending from the district of O'Connell Street and thereabouts. But from the roof no place in particular could be picked out, and we did not know what were the exact houses till people went to town and saw the places for themselves.

Saturday 29 April

On Saturday morning rumours again ran high. Several places had fallen. Jacobs was burned to the ground. Different groups had surrendered. Br Howard had described very graphically the taking of the GPO by the Ulster Volunteers. The Park was in the hands of the Volunteers, he said. The Magazine [Fort] was blown up and, to cap all, 400 Volunteers marching into Dublin from Meath had been ambushed and mown to pieces by machineguns up at Glasnevin. His authorities were Mr. O'Neill, a brother-in-law, and Mrs Foley, a very respectable woman, wife of a DMP [Dublin Metropolitan Policeman]. As soon as we heard the authorities for all these statements, we accepted the wise course and said "Yes, Brother. Good morning".

Following our usual course, we went out on a tour of inspection to see things for ourselves. We went to Ballsbridge and there were held up as we had no military pass. We went down towards Northumberland Road and got as far as Carisbrook House. The house beside the Hammersmith works,[25] owned by Crampton, was badly damaged – windows smashed and wall of the front part and side holed here and there with the bullets fired by the military at the Volunteers. As we passed by we saw the military in the house and at the door. Carisbrook House looked badly knocked about. Windows [were] smashed by the military bullets and the whole place looked a real besieged spot. The military were in the garden, and sentries were all around. Officers were sitting in the parlours taking things easy. We were not allowed to pass, so we got up a laneway and got in to Clyde Road just at the point where I saw the 1st batch of prisoners or suspects taken. All three, I heard, turned out to be ordinary working men and were released afterwards.

Continuing in the same district, Delaney related:

As I came out on the Wellington Road the sentries were just being changed. The Leicesters were doing the work on this road. A sergeant came and spoke to me. He was a Catholic and spoke very highly of Fr O'Rahilly, who had been their chaplain over in England. I was particularly struck by the orders imparted by the corporal to the sentry. "You let nobody pass up, you let nobody pass down, you let nobody pass across without a pass. You've got a rifle and bayonet, you know the rest." This was indeed militarism with a vengeance. I hoped sincerely that none of the poor peaceful citizens of Dublin would fall foul of any of these sentries, for some looked very stupid and very perky little chaps who would use the powers conferred on them very quickly at the smallest provocation. As we stood there, up came a young lad on a bike. He was halted, his pass examined, and allowed to pass. A lady came next, one of the type who had been giving the soldiers tea and cake. She smiled and in her sweetest tone of

CARISBROOK HOUSE, BALLSBRIDGE
An outpost of de Valera's command

voice told the sentry that she wanted to go to the second house from where she stood. "Sorry", said the sentry, "my orders are let nobody pass without a military permit". She smiled and, even in a sweeter tone, said "It is just that house there I want to go to". "Sorry", said the sentry, "my orders are strict". She blushed then and felt very small, especially as we were looking on. She had to retrace her steps. I don't know exactly what she felt, but I know what she looked like.

We passed on and got up to Baggot Street. Some shops were open and doing a very brisk trade, others were closed with a notice in the door that business would be carried on only for a few hours. Prices had gone up. The prices on the articles in the windows were exorbitant. Gents and ladies were doing their own shopping and they were carrying openly vegetables, bread. I smiled at one case. There was a young gent, very fashionably dressed; trying to make up his mind as to which of two legs of lamb he would take, one was 1½ lbs heavier than the other. I did not wait to see what decision he came to. The chemists' shops were under military control. People said the reason was to arrest anyone who came for any kind of medicine to see [if] they were

> connected in any way with the Volunteers.
>
> The front garden of the City of Dublin Hospital was filled with soldiers. They were taking their dinner. So, if any Volunteers fired on them at that moment they couldn't do so without firing at the hospital. Of course, the military had got into Sir Patrick Dunn's Hospital and had fired on the Volunteers stationed in Boland's Mills. This is a solid fact. Two eyewitnesses affirm it. The doctors came out and protested to the military man in charge. We passed up to the canal bridge, where we found several sentries. A crowd had gathered there and was witnessing a fight going on down near Grand Canal Street. The firing was heavy, but I couldn't see anybody except a soldier near Grand Canal Street bridge.

Referring, it seems, to members of the crowd, Delaney proceeded:

> The Protestants were discussing matters and I heard Mr. McNeill's name mentioned several times. There were wild guesses as to what had become of him and as to what was going to happen to him. Mr. McNeill was the head of the Irish Volunteers. He was against the Rising, and would not sign the Proclamation of Independence. Some said the Volunteers had taken him prisoner and held him in the GPO. Others said he was at home in his residence. Others, that he had been arrested by the military. It appeared in the *Irish Times* at the end of the week that he had been arrested, but no further news of him has come as yet.

They continued westward along the canal:

> which was flowing as usual in spite of the troubled state of affairs... We got as far as Charlemont Bridge and found a crowd looking into Charlemont Street. The soldiers were continuing their search through all the houses. I spoke to a few people. They all assured me that Jacobs was still standing, and to confirm this shots rang out in that direction. I was not content with mere hearsay. I found one who had passed by and he assured me the Volunteers were still in possession. As I was not allowed across Portobello [bridge], I turned my steps Rathmineswards and passed up by the barracks. The military were still on guard and all around about looked as if in a state of siege. The sol-

diers were hiding behind walls, trees, door posts etc, ready to fire at the first sign. St Mary's Catholic College had been taken and occupied by the military. The staff of Holy Ghost Fathers were asked to leave. It is said also, I have not first hand proof, that the military occupied the dome of the Rathmines Catholic Church. All said it, so I give it for what it is worth. I did not see the soldiers there, but that wouldn't prove anything, as they have learned a lesson from exposing themselves in the steeple of Haddington Road Church.

We passed up along the Rathmines Road, and just as we came to the Town Hall out dashed the fire-brigade car and flew off in the direction of Milltown. It turned out to be the public house in the village of Milltown that was on fire. The firemen soon had the flames under control and then left for the fire station. But as soon as the firemen had departed, the villagers looted the house as there was nobody in it and above all no policemen to be seen, as all the DMP were in barracks and were not allowed to stir out. One of them told me, "Begorra, Father, I was quite happy that I hadn't to go out, for had I gone I'd be a dead man by this".

Well, when the fire-brigade car passed us, we crossed the Rathmines Road and went up along the Leinster Road and had a good look at Countess Markievicz's house. The door was open and inside was a table with something like bandages on it. A huge red flag or something of that description was on the ground. The whole house had something of a dishevelled appearance. There were no sentries to be seen and all seemed quite peaceful. We passed on and got out on the Harold's Cross Road. Things seemed peaceful enough. The only strange feature was the kind of people doing their shopping and carrying food quite ostensibly. We got as far as the canal bridge where the soldiers were engaged in pulling down the hoarding for bill posting. This was in order that the soldiers in Wellington Barracks [now Cathal Brugha Barracks] could have a clear sweep of all the roads leading to the bridge. I met one soldier who seemed a hardened veteran. He asked me to post a photo for him. It was for his mother in South Africa. He feared he would be killed and that he would not be able to forward the photo to her. He belonged

> to the South African Infantry. "How did you get here," I asked him. "Well I was through the whole Boer War on the British side. I was through the late rebellion on Botha's side and then, when that was over, I volunteered for service in France. We were sent to England for three months training, and I was over in Ireland on 7 days leave when the insurrection broke out. So I got orders to join my regiment and thus you see me here." He looked a very solid individual and stood out in a wonderful way when compared with the ordinary Tommies. As it looked very dangerous along the canal, we returned home.
>
> On the way, as we were passing a side street, there was a shout. "God bless you Father, Mary here is a parent at last." I turned and saw three poor women. One had a large basket filled with plants, another carried a little baby, and the other had a little cart filled with greens. They ran after us. "Bless us, Father", said the poor things. "We'll be shot this evening. There is dreadful work in our court, soldiers and Volunteers killing one another."

Delaney, conscious that he was not yet a priest, relayed his reaction to this:

> They looked very frightened, and I thought it better to make a sign of the cross on their foreheads. That will do no harm, I thought. Some of the "haw, haw" inhabitants looked on. They did not even smile, and the poor women went off calling down all the blessings of heaven on us and on themselves for having the good fortune of meeting us.

He continues his account:

> As we came into Ranelagh, I met one of our men talking to young O'Rahilly. He had some bits of scraps of news. It appeared that The O'Rahilly[26] had sent his wife a note that morning to say they were abandoning the GPO. The military had dropped incendiary bombs on the building and had set it on fire. [He also stated] that the Volunteers were in grand form and had no idea of surrender.
>
> We got home to dinner and heard most extraordinary accounts of all the scenes of fighting. After dinner, I left for Ballsbridge direction and found huge crowds passing to and fro across the

Sackville Street (O'Connell Street)

As Seen From One Of The Houses On The West Side

General Post Office (GPO), Sackville Street

"Loyal Volunteers on duty at GPO – Military passing."

bridge. The soldiers seemed to be quite happy and were very friendly with the people. There was a great crowd round the Town Hall looking for military passes. Rumours were abroad that all the Volunteers had surrendered. Some were happy. Others were of opinion that it was a pity that they had come to such an abrupt end. We asked several soldiers. They replied they knew nothing about it. I met two sergt. majors. I asked them. "We heard nothing about it." The firing was still going on in the direction of Boland's Mills. I met a young officer. I put the same question to him. "I know nothing about it." And yet all seemed to be quite happy that the whole thing was over. Staff officers were swanking about, and as one drove off in his motor, a tall Protestant minister bid him good bye, adding "Sorry you are going and that your work is over so soon". That seemed to be in favour of a surrender. I met two Catholic chaplains and asked them. They knew nothing about it and heard nothing official about the surrender. I couldn't make head or tale of all the reports.

As we were talking to the Catholic chaplains up came the Non-Conformist chaplain, who gave us an insight to his mind and religious belief in a very few sentences. "You know I am the Non-Conformist chaplain, but I can take on any service. I take the Baptist, the Low Church, the High Church, in fact any service you wish. I was taken several times for a Catholic chaplain. My wife is Irish, so the Volunteers won't touch me." "Well", I said, "you had better write that across your uniform". He told us so many stories about his life since the war began. He was in Salonika, France, and now in Ireland. We gathered [that] his mind was so broad in religious matters as to admit of very many contradictions.

As we were talking up came 3 or 4 old Protestant ladies of the real sourface type. "Oh, here are the chaplains", they said. "Are you going to hold service tomorrow", one asked. "I don't think there will be any parade service", said the Non-Conformist parson. "There may be a voluntary service." "Will you hold it at St Bartholomew's [the High Church]?" "I'm afraid not", said the Catholic chaplains, "as there are no High Church chaplains with us." You should have seen their faces when they heard this. "Oh", chimed in the Non-Conformist parson, "if they wish I can hold the service for them, for I can pray anywhere. I prayed in Catholic churches when I was in France" – a good reason why, I said to myself, though I did not say it to him, was that there were no Non-Conformist churches there or so very few that he could not find them. We bid him Good Evening, and as he was leaving he said – "Well, I may become an RC yet".

We passed down by the Royal Dublin Society's buildings. We met a fine looking officer standing on the foot-path. This one perhaps may tell us something of the surrender. "I know nothing at all", he replied to our question, "but I doubt it very much. Do you hear all the firing going on. That does not look much like surrender". Then he unburdened himself. "I pity those poor fellows", he said. "Will they be shot, those who surrender?" I asked. "The mind of the army is that they should not be shot", he said. "My opinion is that these poor fellows have been misled. Now tell me," he said, turning right round on us, "You ought to know. Would it be right for me to say that the reason why these rose and took up arms against us was that they disbelieved the Government, that all the promises made by the Government would not be carried out ?" "Certainly", we said, "that was the essence of all their publications and statements. Had Home Rule been granted this would never have occurred for it would not be possible." "Now I held that all along", he said, "but I was told I was wrong. And you know they had a good reason to disbelieve the Government the way it had been going on with its wait and see policy and let things work themselves out." "You know", he continued, "the Government is rotten. Its nothing but a pack of old women. Just like the army. The army is rotten also. Now just look at that fellow", he said, pointing to a young officer, "I could be his grandfather. Not that I object to young men being placed over me, far from it, provided they have brains – but look at that fellow", he said, pointing to the young officer again, "sure stupidity is patent in his very face." And I must say I had to agree with him, especially as regards superior officers and, above all, the staff officers, some of whom were mere boys, with nothing remarkable on their countenance except the absence of all signs of ability.

We bid our friend Good Evening, and were just asking ourselves what we could believe about the whole matter, when suddenly a shot rang out and there was a scamper amongst the military. All the faces wore changed expressions. All the joy and delight disappeared and consternation was painted on the faces of military and civilians. Orders rang out. Rifles were swung round from the soldiers' shoulders ready to fire. The sentries presented fixed bayonets to the crowds around the different gates. The shot had rung out from the Serpentine Avenue. The soldiers made towards this area, dropped on their knees, some on their stomachs, others behind walls. Shots rang out, a section of fully armed and fully equipped soldiers came up at the double with rifles in their hands ready to fire. The officer was not at their head but in the middle of the section and surrounded by the soldiers, looking more like a prisoner than the head or leader of the section. The ambulance was sent for and flew down Serpentine Avenue. In a few minutes it came back with a respectably dressed man lying on one of the stretchers.

The ambulance flew off towards the Royal Dublin Society's buildings. As the man was being taken out of the ambulance, there was a dreadful shout. I could not hear exactly what was said. Some say he wished to escape and made endeavours. Others say he thought he was going to be shot and asked for mercy as he was being carried into the hall. Whatever he said, one thing is certain, the poor soldiers got awfully scared and cleared the crowd with fixed bayonets. One Protestant gentleman and lady said, in my hearing, "I hope they'll shoot that man." "Oh", I said, "are you Germans?" "Oh, no," replied the lady looking frightened at the question. I suppose she thought I might hand her over to the military. My question had the desired effect. She kept quiet and said no more. We thought it better to move off, as I did not wish to taste any cold steel just at that moment. So I turned my steps homewards.

We were met by many who asked us "Did the Volunteers surrender?" We gave them the answer we had received, "We don't know". The testimony of our senses, especially our ears, was against all the reports of surrender, for machine guns were rattling away in all directions over the city. We met one lady, who solemnly affirmed that Fr Moloney of Donnybrook had received a telephone message from the Castle to say that Pearse had surrendered. Just as she announced this, the rattle of the machine guns increased so we refused to accept her report. We returned home and found that reports of surrender had got there also, but the firing was very heavy and, as happened the other days, we did not know what to believe.

What happened actually at Ballsbridge just as I left was told to me by an eye witness, who was held as prisoner inside the Show Grounds the whole night. The soldiers, who had come up to the Serpentine Avenue, began to search the terrace of houses. Just as the military had completed this operation they were fired on from behind, the shots coming from the grounds of the female Masonic school at the corner of the road. The officer did not know what to do, seeing he was taken in the rear, and thinking above all they [the Volunteers] had occupied this school. It turned out afterwards that it was one solitary sniper who was giving all this trouble. He had secreted himself in the bushes round about the grounds. The soldiers withdrew in order to get around the terrace and school [and they became] massed in front of the Dublin Society's buildings. As soon as they got into this position, fire was opened on them from the dispensary in front of the Town Hall, and thus the military were caught on three (?) sides and suffered very heavily. They had been caught napping, and were badly trapped: their very headquarters attacked and their officers around the building fell. This fight went on till after 10.00pm, and the only Volunteer caught was the one in the Masonic school grounds. Some say that it was a machine gun they [the Volunteers] had in the dispensary. But it does not seem to be certain, though the number of shots fired seemed to come from something like a machine gun.

Naturally, the sentries became rather strict around about Ballsbridge. The people who were hemmed in about the Show Grounds were kept there till 5.00am on Sunday. Some were in a dreadful state, naturally enough, thinking their last moments had come. Of course, the reports that spread about the Ballsbridge fight were really novelistic. I had to wait till I got the above details from an eye witness, who had passed the night – forcibly of course – in the Show Grounds. One thing was certain, that the firing throughout that Saturday and Sunday morning was very heavy, and that consequently it was clear that there was no surrender yet, at least in these parts.

Sunday, 30 April 1916

On Sunday I went off towards Ranelagh, but we could not advance very far on the Ranelagh Road. Sentries were placed and nobody was allowed to pass without a permit. Dr Johnson was out with his Red Cross band on his arm, ready, I suppose, to render medical aid to the first who needed it. We went down towards Leeson Street and found the military in possession there also. There was a group around Cullen's shop. There we got more information, namely that a medical [doctor] had been down to St Vincent's Hospital and saw the republican flag floating over the College of Surgeons at 9.30 that morning. So there was no surrender at that hour, that was certain. Now came the next [news], which seemed to contradict the message that Fr O'Brien had received from his brother the evening before that "all were in grand form and that there was no idea of any surrender". Well, Mr. Cullen said that a Protestant minister had passed by coming from town and [had] announced that he had seen with his own eyes about 100 men march out of the College of Surgeons and surrender, and that they had been marched to the Castle. That seemed evidence, and first hand.

However, I still had some doubts. As I stood there I saw a DMP come over the bridge from town riding a bike. He did look a strange being as we had not seen a policeman for such a long time. This looked like peace now. All people passing the bridge were stopped, and those who had no papers were sent back. The military had occupied the house at the corner and anyone who was suspect was sent in there to be examined by the officer in charge. As I was speaking, up came a van driven by a

SURRENDERING
Éamon de Valera leading his command from Bolands, escorted by British soldiers

very respectable looking man. It was evident he was not an ordinary van man. He had two large Red Cross flags flying from the corner of his van. Mr. Cullen told us that the man was Mr. Fitzsimons, who was going around the town with this van collecting the dead bodies and bringing them to the different cemeteries. He ran great personal risks on this work of mercy and deserves great praise as he had to pass through many danger zones.

We went down Morehampton Road and passed the military headquarters of the district, which was a private house commandeered by the military. As we reached this, more troops were coming into town. I was watching them. They looked bewildered. As they passed empty houses they cast very ominous looks towards the windows and doors as if they expected a few pieces of lead from these spots. Nothing happened while I was there. We passed on and met Brother Howard, who told us that 300 men, with de Valera at their head, had surrendered at Boland's and had just marched up along the Pembroke Road to Ballsbridge Show Grounds, where the military had their headquarters. Crowds had witnessed this march of the surrendered commander. Of course, the Volunteers were in high spirits and whistled Irish airs, and especially marches, as they swung along, surrounded by soldiers carrying fixed bayonets. They were searched at Ballsbridge and then sent into the Show Grounds, where they were kept as prisoners till they were removed to Richmond Barracks up near Inchicore.

I was very sorry I had not been down to see them, but I couldn't see everything. We went down through Herbert Park. There I heard from others who saw the prisoners march in. The numbers, however, began to change. One said 300, others said 100, others 150. So I took the mean and accepted that about 150 had surrendered. All spoke very highly of young de Valera, professor in Blackrock College. He displayed real military genius in dispersing his men in real strategical points. They had taken over all the buildings of importance and then placed outposts to guard all the approaches. One of his cleverest tricks, for he had several, was to place the republican flag on the old distillery. This drew all the heavy fire and not a single Volunteer was in it. So all the shells were going for naught. How he brought up his ammunition was brilliant. He had a canal boat filled as it were with turf. When they took possession of Bolands, he sent out his men to remove the top sods ... and low and behold they found a canal boat full of ammunition, and this had passed along the canal quite innocently. The manager of Boland's told me that de Valera was a fine young fellow, had his men well under control, would not allow them to do any harm to anything unless what was absolutely necessary for the defence of the place, so much so that the machinery was left untouched, the safe left as it was, the flour and bread was left where it was, and the only thing they did was use that which they needed for themselves.

I then made my way home, coming across a young man who gave us a great description of the Ballsbridge fight the night before. As I went into Donnybrook I saw all the people making their way to devotions. It was strange. Martial law changed even the hours for evening devotions and great crowds flocked. I suppose a number wanted to make up for their Mass that morning, as they were afraid to leave their homes on account of the stray bullets. I met a man who had been arrested and detained for a few hours by the military. He had nothing to do with the movement at all, but was detained as a suspect. I looked at him and listened to his story, and then said to myself "Well you, my poor fellow, wouldn't do any harm to anybody", but he did look a bit battered and knocked about. I returned home to all kinds of stories about the surrender.

One had managed to get across to different parts of the town. And he had eye-witness accounts so things seemed to be more or less certain now. He had passed by the College of Surgeons and found the military taking all kinds of stuff out of the college.[27] He had passed along to the Castle and had spoken to an officer, who stated that about 100 prisoners had marched down to the Castle from the College of Surgeons with the Countess at their head. She was dressed in male attire. He had passed up then to Jacob's factory in Camden Street and saw the Volunteers throw out some flour to the people as it was announced that they had surrendered. The Four Courts had also given in, as the gates were open. Such evidence seemed to be conclusive, and we all accepted the statement that all had surrendered.

We went in for our visit to the Blessed Sacrament, when the rifle fire increased again and all the evidence seemed to be thrown to the winds again. But we agreed and believed that they must be detached bodies, who were still holding out and to whom the news could not reach of the general surrender of the Volunteers.

NOTES

1. Milltown Park Archives. A press containing a journal giving 'Ordinations since 1906'
2. John Delaney papers, Irish Jesuit Archives (IJA), J29/3/5/1-8
3. John's sister Johanna was 28 in 1916. Harry is not identified. He was perhaps a resident in the house, or a boyfriend of John's sister, or a colleague or friend of John's.
4. Rotunda refers to the Rotunda Hospital at the end of O'Connell Street, beyond the Parnell statue.
5. St Stephen's Green, Jacob's biscuit factory, the Phoenix Park.
6. Fr Francis Xavier O'Brien SJ (1881–1974) was ordained in 1915, just a year before John Delaney. He was subsequently to serve as a chaplain in the Great War, 1917–1918. He spent almost the rest of his life in Australia, which was part of the Irish Jesuit province until 1931/2.

7. IJA J 29/3/6
8. Guinness Brewery, St James's Gate, Dublin
9. Fr James McCann SJ (1875–1951) was a stockbroker before becoming a Jesuit in 1899. Ordained in 1911, he was bursar and administrator of temporal matters in Milltown Park during 1916. He served as a chaplain in France, 1917–1919, and went into Germany with the occupying troops. He received the Military Cross.
10. The Nottingham & Derbyshire Regiment. The Sherwood Foresters.
11. IJA. Section J 29/3/7
12. Fr Tom Finlay SJ (1848–1940) was once described by the Irish Independent as perhaps 'the best known man in Ireland'. He was a noted educationist, editor, professor, and social reformer. In University College Dublin, under the Royal University of Ireland and then the National University of Ireland, he lectured, in turn, in classics, philosophy, and economics. He was the co-founder of the Irish Agricultural Co-operative Society.
13. 'Mrs Carew' was a celebrated religious sister of the Irish Sisters of Charity. Mary Bernard Carew (1869–1954) was a nurse in St Vincent's Hospital from 1893–1918, and from 1905 was matron and superior of the religious community attached to the hospital. In the 1920s she returned to the position of matron and continued until 1935, when she was elected superior general of the congregation. She was a capable and formidable lady, who became a legend in medical circles.
14. Fr John Hannon SJ (1884–1947) was ordained in 1915, the year before Delaney. He was to go on to lecture in philosophy and theology and to become rector of Milltown Park. Later he was elected to the position of assistant to the Father General of the order.
15. 'Brunswick Street', or as it was known Greater Brunswick Street, was the street in which Padraig Pearse, leader of the 1916 Rising, was born. Dublin Corporation in 1920 re-named Brunswick Street after the executed leader, Pearse Street.
16. Fr Jack Byrne (1888–1919) was a curate in Cullenswood parish and lived quite near to Milltown Park in Beechwood Avenue, Ranelagh. He served in Rathmines, 1915–1918.
17. Francis Sheehy-Skeffington was a very well known figure in Dublin literary and reforming circles. He opposed violence and strongly supported women's rights. He was murdered in 1916 by a seemingly unbalanced British officer, Captain Bowen-Colethurst.
18. Thomas McDonagh was a lecturer in English at University College Dublin, a poet, and active Volunteer. He was one of the signatories of the Proclamation of the Irish Republic and was executed in 1916. His wife, nee Muriel Gifford, was tragically drowned while swimming at Skerries, Co Dublin, a year later, on 9 July 1917.
19. The Irish Volunteers were founded in 1912 in response to the foundation of the Ulster Volunteers opposed to Home Rule. Subsequently, the Irish Volunteers split into the National Volunteers, who followed the leadership of John Redmond, MP, leader of the Irish Parliamentary Party, and the remainder who retained the name Irish Volunteers.
20. Sir Mathew Nathan was under-secretary to the Lord Lieutenant or Viceroy of Ireland, Lord Wimborne, 1914–1916
21. Judge Johnson's house has evaded identification. The traceable judges of that name lived in a different area.
22. The town of Kut-al-Amara, in present day Iraq, was held by British forces and was besieged by Turkish troops from December 1915 to April 1916. The garrison capitulated on 29 April 1916. The siege evoked much interest. The capitulation was viewed as a serious setback to Britain's military reputation.
23. IJA J 29/3/8

24. 'Subs' – Subalterns, officers below the rank of captain.

25. The Hamersmith Works, Ballsbridge, became a celebrated iron foundry in the 19th century under Richard Turner. His constructions were well known in Britain and Ireland, e.g., the great Botanical Glass House in Kew. The business closed down in 1876. Much of the extensive site is currently occupied by the eight storey Hume House offices, Pembroke Road, Ballsbridge. The reference to Crampton's house, was to the house of a celebrated Dublin master builder. Carisbrook House was a very fine, well known building, which was occupied by the Volunteers for a short time during the rising.

26. The O'Rahilly was a member of the Irish Republican Brotherhood (IRB) and a founding figure of the Irish Volunteers. The prefix to a name was a Gaelic designation referring to the senior living descendant of the chieftain of a clan – (Dorothy Macardle. *The Irish Republic,* 1958 ed., p. 90 f.n.). The O'Rahilly may have been a self-appointed chieftain.

27. IJA J 29/3/9

ARCHBISHOP'S HOUSE,
WESTMINSTER, S.W.

May 3rd, 1915.

Dear Father Provincial,

There is now a very urgent need for another large increase in the number of Priests to do duty as Chaplains in the Army or Navy. Would you very kindly let me know if you have any Fathers available whom you can specially recommend as in every way suitable for these duties. I should be grateful if you would be good enough to state in each case if the Father prefers one of the Services to the other, so that I may be able, if possible, to satisfy this preference. Any Priest accepted for duty of this kind must be at the disposition of H. M.'s Government until the end of the War.

Believe me, dear Father Provincial,

Your devoted servant in Christ,

Francis Cardinal Bourne

Delegate of the Holy See for the British Army & Navy.

Request from Cardinal Francis Bourne, Archbishop of Westminster to Father Provincial Thomas V. Nolan SJ, seeking chaplains in the Army and Navy. May 3rd 1915.
Reference: IJA/CHP1/1

Chapter 3

'On the plains of death'

Military Chaplain 1917–1919

Ordination as priest

In the weeks after the Rising, John, like most of the population, was perturbed and then angered by the execution of the leading figures in the insurrection and the imprisonment of hundreds of others who had no part in it. But, understandably, his main focus was on his ordination to the priesthood. It was the goal towards which he had directed his life and long training. His father had not lived to see him and his colleagues ordained at Milltown Park on 31 July 1916. But his mother was present with other members of his family. In the weeks after ordination he became accustomed to celebrating Mass in various places. Then, it was back to study for his final year of theology.

Responding to the needs of war

During these years reports on the Great War filled the newspapers. The litany of deaths was a reminder of the importance of military chaplains to comfort and assist the thousands of Catholic soldiers. Irrespective of political or other considerations, John's thoughts, like those of many of his fellow Jesuits, turned towards chaplaincy. The Irish Jesuit archives indicate that the provincial, Fr T.V. Nolan, forwarded John's name to Cardinal Bourne of Westminster, who directed the appointment of

FR WILLIE DOYLE SJ

"I came across remnants of the famous 16th Division the other day. They were full of Father Doyle and his exploits. How grieved they are at his sad loss..."

Catholic chaplains to the British Expeditionary Force in France. On 20 July, Monsignor Michael Bidwell thanked Fr Nolan for John's application, requested his medical certificate, and observed that there was a great shortage of priests. There were 60 vacancies in France. On 31 July 1917, John completed the various documents for appointment. He gave his age as 34 years, and on his 'clerical experience' he wrote that he had been chaplain to the 'Royal Hospital for Incurables and to the King George V Hospital [military]'. He furnished a letter from the stipulated doctor. This testified to his ability to discharge the duties of a military chaplain, adding that 'he had been in the East [Ceylon] for some years and while there contracted an attack of dysentery of which he has long times been completely free'.[1]

Notification reached him on 13 August 1917 that he had been selected 'as a temporary chaplain to the Forces with the British Expeditionary Force in France'.[2] He signed the conditions of service two days later. He gave as his next of kin, the Jesuit provincial, Rev. T.V. Nolan SJ, and his sister, Mrs H. Brennan, 10 Charlemont Terrace, Malahide Road, Clontarf, Dublin.[3] Things moved quickly after that. On 22 August, he was instructed to embark at Folkstone on Thursday, 28th. The first train on that date left London, Victoria Station, at 7.35am.[4]

As he set out, John was conscious of being part of a long tradition. Jesuits had served as military chaplains from the earliest years of the Society of Jesus. More than 30 Irish Jesuits were to serve as chaplain in the First World War. Already, one of them had become very well known. Fr Willie Doyle, attached to the 16th Division, Royal Dublin Fusiliers, had taken risks few other chaplains matched in treating the wounded and the dying. His name was mentioned in numerous despatches, and he was awarded the Military Cross. He was killed at Ypres on 17 August 1917, just eleven days before John set out for France. Widely mourned by his Division and also by the 36th Ulster Division, Fr Doyle's death received much publicity in the press. His example was not lost on John Delaney.

Letters from France and Flanders

Delaney's first extant letter to Fr Nolan came from France. It was undated, but was probably sent early in September:

> I have just got into my quarters. I am stationed with the ar-

> tillery of the 50th Division... The officers are all very decent fellows, though very few are Catholics. We had Mass last Sunday for my area in the YMCA [Young Men's Christian Association] tent. We had over 250 present and about 150 communions. We preached – "just a few feeling words". We have some Americans here also, working on the railways etc. The Bosche planes pay us frequent visits and the "archies" – name given to the anti-aircraft guns – give them a warm welcome. I had my first battle on Sunday eve. It is glorious yet terrible. The sight is a bit theatrical, but when you begin to think of what it means the reality is then dreadful. Poor fellows, they have a very hard time of it.

Delaney expressed his regret that he was unable to meet with the provincial before he left. He got orders on the Thursday night and had to leave on Saturday night. He had gone to Gardiner Street to see Fr Nolan but learnt that he was out. In his Division, Delaney explained, there were three Jesuits and he met four others.[5]

On 23 September, he wrote to express sympathy with the provincial on the death of his brother. He had just read of it in the newspaper. He added:

> I came across remnants of the famous 16th Division the other day. They were full of Father Doyle and his exploits. How grieved they are at his sad loss nobody can tell unless they speak to them personally. He seemed to have gripped them all, individually as well as collectively.

'I have plenty of work and more opening up', Delaney explained, 'units who have not seen a priest for ages.'[6]

His final extant letter to Fr Nolan was from Flanders, on 6 December 1917. He asked the provincial's approval to spend his leave in 'dear old Dublin', and described the conditions in Flanders:

> It is a hot front up here and the wonder is how so many come through in spite of shell and bomb. The poor artillery are always in [sic] and it is a strain on the poor fellows to be always at it, especially up here. The mud is respectable during these days as the frost has stiffened it up a bit, but then the thaw! And a thaw in Flanders, and that with artillery! So we have grand prospects!

He met several of the English Jesuit Province at the army chaplains' meeting, but there were none from Ireland. There were a number of diocesan priests, among them Fr Gleeson of the Dublin diocese.[7] Things were 'becoming more organised now, but the work that remains to be done!' (The initial organisation on the part of the War Office had been chaotic). He concluded by asking the provincial's remembrance at Mass for him and his work.[8]

John Delaney's thoughts returned often to St Aloysius College, Ceylon. His most frequent and detailed letters were to the superior of the mission, Fr Olivier Feron. A number of these were published in the college magazine, *The Aloysian,* during 1917 and 1918, under the title 'Father Delaney at the Front'. They have been made available courtesy of the present editor, John de Silva. Delaney's first letter to Fr Feron was from France, dated 15 September 1917:

> Dear Father Superior,
>
> I suppose you will be somewhat surprised to get these few lines from the above address. I am in the army now and out at the front… I am attached to the artillery… My present address is the 1st Sect DAC 50th Division BEF France. I volunteered and left myself in Fr Proces's hands. He put me at the disposal of Father T.V. Nolan, the Irish Provincial, and here I am. The appeals that were going forth were too strong. I, at least, said "whatever the superiors think, I don't know, but I shall place myself in their hands", and I don't think you will say I did wrong or even "*moins bien*". The mission's demand was great and a very serious obstacle, I saw that, but, as they said, the urgent need and the need of the moment was for priests at the front...
>
> I got orders on Thursday evening and had to be in France on the following Tuesday... Our camp is not so large at present but we are moving. I say Mass in my tent each morning. It is rather a sentimental thing at first, especially when you realise what it all means, and then see the surroundings, but is it not further proof of His love for us?
>
> I say Mass on Sunday in the YMCA marquee or in a cinema show room. We have about 300 present and 50 or 60 communions some mornings. I have a few who go up to the lines that day, who get confession and receive communion in my tent. We

CHP1/12 (1)

Thursday

Dear Fr Provincial

I have just got into my quarters. I am stationed with the Artillery of the 50th Div. I live with the 2nd Sect. of the D.A.C. The Officers are all very decent fellows. though

I

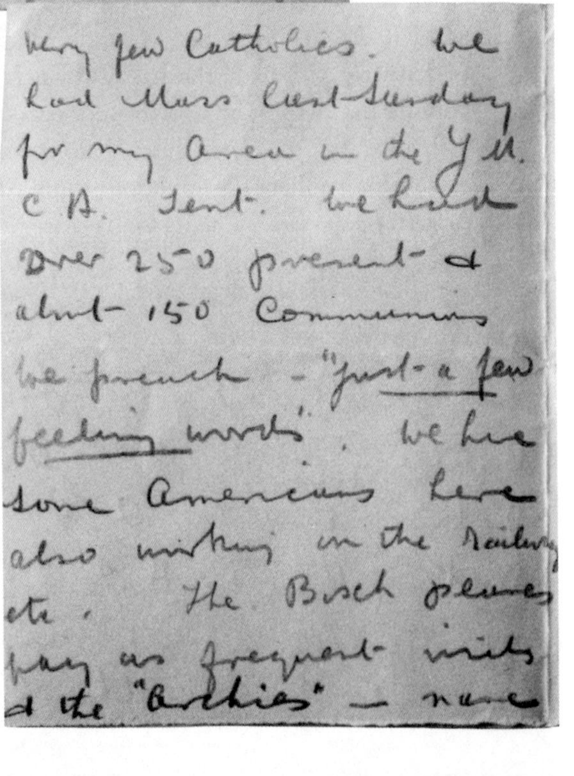

very few Catholics. We had Mass last Sunday for my Area in the Y.M. C.A. Tent. We had over 250 present & about 150 Communions. We preach – "just a few feeling words". We have some Americans here also working on the railway etc. The Bosch planes pay us frequent visits & the "Archies" – name

II

FOUR PAGES OF A LETTER FROM JOHN DELANEY SJ TO THE PROVINCIAL FR T.V. NOLAN

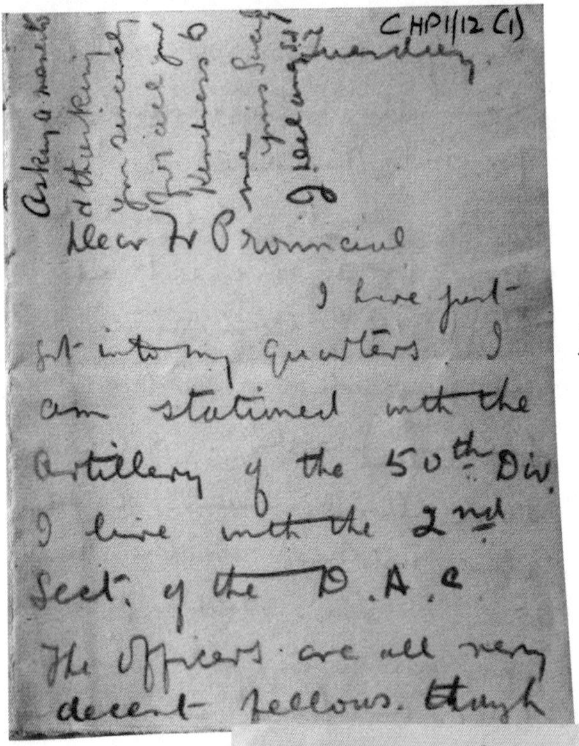

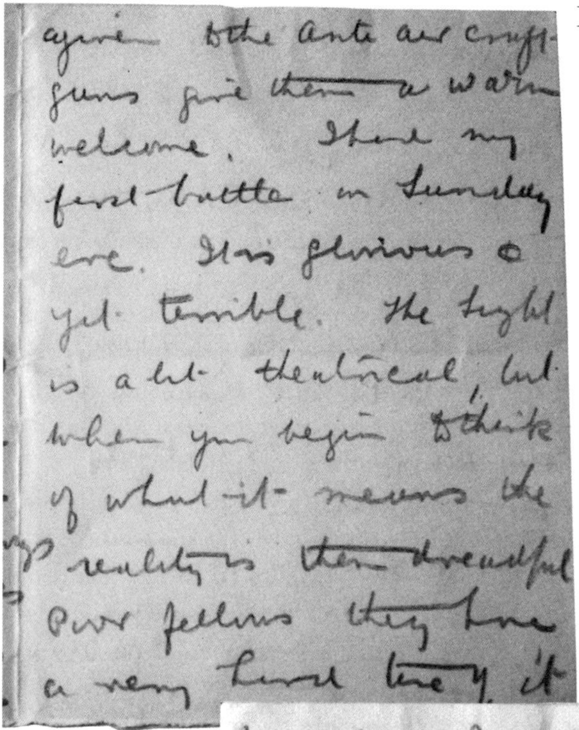

III

again to the Anti air craft
guns give them a warm
welcome. I had my
first battle on Sunday
eve. It is glorious &
yet terrible. The sight
is a bit theatrical, but
when you begin to think
of what it means the
reality is then dreadful
Poor fellows they have
a very hard time of it

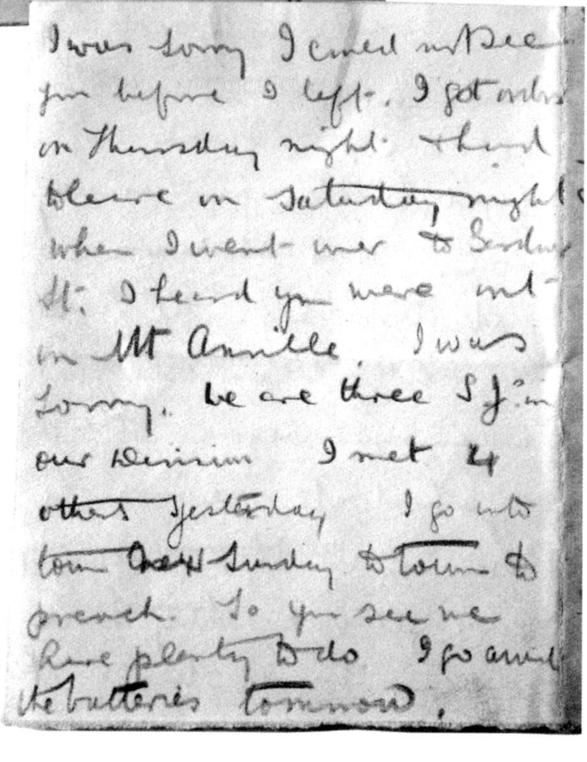

I was sorry I could not see
you before I left. I got orders
on Thursday night. I had
to leave on Saturday night
when I went over to Sandy
St: I heard you were out
in Mt Anville. I was
sorry. We are three S.J. in
our Division I met 4
others yesterday. I go into
town next Sunday to town to
preach. So you see we
have plenty to do. I go round
the batteries tomorrow.

IV

are fairly quiet at present. The only things to disturb us are the Boche planes that come hovering over our camps, with – well, not very pleasant designs. The moment they are spotted, then begins the fun. The anti-aircraft guns, or as the men call them, the "archies", begin to pop. The only danger for us is bits of shell coming flying about. The other morning the bits were flying in all directions around about the tent in which I was saying Mass. I had my first experience of battle a few days ago… The bursting and banging of the shells, added to the many colours of the different lights, then the smoke and the bursting of shells overhanging the trenches and the yelling and shouting of the men: It is really glorious, quite theatrical even, if you could only forget the consequences, and these are terrible!

One Irish lad was brought in, in a very bad condition. He was anointed and prepared for death. "Am I going to die, Father?" asked the poor lad. You are not allowed to tell them. "Well now, my poor fellow, put yourself in our Lord's hands; He will look after you; you couldn't be in better, could you?" "Ah! Sure Father, I know that," was his quick reply, but that young lad was laid to rest two days after. He was the only son of a poor Irish widowed mother. That is when the reality of war comes home to you, when you see such cases as that.

The desolation and ruin on all sides are really dreadful. The Boche knows how to level down. Villages are nothing more than bricks and mortar; churches share the same fate as the humble cottages, but, strange to say, the crucifixes are standing everywhere. It is a most pathetic sight to look across a vast plain to see a few crucifixes standing erect amidst such desolation and ruin. I have been in several of these ruined churches. In some, altars remain; in others you will find only a statue in a small niche. In others you will have to inquire whether it was a church or a large hall, for all the traces are gone; and not merely is it small village churches that have suffered so, but town churches and even cathedrals have been dealt with in the same drastic method.

I was on my rounds the other day amongst the batteries. This is my work. There they were shelling the Boches the whole afternoon. It is dreadful to think of it all. I had a peep through a telescope and, right enough, there were the Germans passing to and fro along a road. Just as I was gazing, bang went one shell, then another, followed by a third and a fourth right on our trenches. The poor fellows underneath them! But you have moments of real consolation. Last night we had a real turn out in the neighbouring town. I was invited to preach, we had the usual duties and after the sermon we had a procession of the Blessed Sacrament. There were up to 300 men in uniform marching and singing the hymn "Jesus, my Lord, my God, my all." It did good to everybody, priests as well as soldiers. There were a few French nuns present. The tears filled their eyes at such a sight. It was really glorious.

You see our lives are strange, in fact very strange. You should see me, washing outside my tent door in the mornings, or getting into my sleeping bag at night to lie down in my camp bed. Bro Polydore would enjoy it all. I must get a photo taken and send it to you. I am sure you will all laugh heartily when you see me in my captain's uniform, but if you saw me with my gas mask and shell helmet on, I think you would do anything but smile. We look frights, we really do. Well Fr Superior, *au revoir,* don't forget to say and to have said a few prayers for me and for my work. I am sure the boys won't forget me. All AMDG [*Ad majorem Dei gloriam* – to God's greater glory, the Jesuit motto], and you will see Galle blessed for the momentary sacrifice of one of its members.

From Flanders on 13th November, in a long letter, Delaney provided a vivid picture of a chaplain's life at the front. In the process, he described earlier events as he and his men were sent on a long mysterious journey, which brought them from France to Flanders. Unwittingly, they were part of the series of encounters called generally the battle of Passchendaele, which was waged, from 31 July to 10 November 1917, east of Ypres, in Southwest Belgium. It was a conflict marked by an intense and massive bombardment that inflicted damage on the land drains and, combined with the unseasonable heavy rainfall, turned the battlefield into a quagmire where men drowned in shell holes. Delaney, like most officers and men, had no idea of the wider picture, nor of the immense number of casualties in that particular conflict, nor that it had resulted in the deaths of two such well known Irish personalities as Willie Redmond, MP, and Tom Kettle, professor of economics, former member of parliament, orator and poet – one of his poems, written the day before he was killed, became one of the better known poems of the war. It evoked some of Delaney's own views on the war and the service of others.[9] Delaney's attention, meantime, was focussed on the immediate situation and on the spiritual and material welfare of his men.

Flanders, November 13th, 1917

Dear Father Superior,

A very happy and a very merry X'mas to all from my little dug-out in the West. It is a charming and most picturesque abode of peace; this same dug-out situated on the side of a ditch, hollowed out of the ground about 2ft with sand bags to complete the wall. Poles on either end connected with a beam form the frame work of the roof, which is a cart cover. The ground is dry – a real marvel – due principally to the nice little brick fire-place I built. My bed! Such a grandiose name for the affair that serves that purpose for me. Well, it is a trench board on which my bed valise is stretched. ... The one great drawback is, we can't stand erect. So I am on my knees many and many a time.

Well, such is the abode in Flanders, whence the good X'mas wishes issue to travel across the miles of ocean to old Ceylon. I hope all are quite well and that I get a few prayers from time to time, for we want them all. Remember me very specially to all the members of the community. As you can see, we are not in the same position as we were when I wrote to you last. Since then we have been on the trek. It is a strange life for us, when you pause and think. I thought so the night we left our last camp.

There we were, all drawn up along the road, ready for inspection. I was mounted on my charger and looked just as bloodthirsty as the rest. Khaki does give you the appearance, in the twilight especially, when you are fully buttoned and properly buckled up. Well, we passed all right and the order rang out and off we went to – God knows where!... We got off that

© The Father Browne Collection

PREPARING TO ADVANCE
Passchendaele, Flanders, 1917

evening and passed through a great number of French villages, the inhabitants of which must be heartily sick of all this rolling along of gun carriages and wagons. We got into a very nice little town and all went to sleep, accustomed to the dreadful noises of war.

We then entrained. Such a scene! The dead of night, not a light, but the noise! Such shouting and the choice and poetic language the Tommy knows how to use! The horses and mules had to be watered and fed before entraining, and bringing them to the troughs meant stepping into mud-holes up to your knees in slush; yet all went with a swing, and even the most obstinate mule was entrained with the help of ropes and above all the choicest expressions of the most poetic language, and soon we were puffing along, having deluded Fritz once more. Each one got a corner and made the best of it, something in the style of the night mail to and from N'Eliya. All I know is that when I awoke we were still "somewhere in France," exactly where I didn't know myself. One thing was certain, we were puffing along. No chance of saying Mass that morning, the second I missed since I came to France. The cookers were soon going, and with some hot water from the engine, we boiled eggs and even poached those, the shells of which had been cracked, and breakfast was served *a la Tommy.* You really enjoy that kind of meal more than any served in the regular mess.

The train kept puffing along the whole time and brought us past French troops and British, all of whom seemed to be anxious to know what division that was and where we were bound for. The Australians gave us a great nod of the head and shouted "cheery ho!" They are great lads, great fighters and great workers and great soldiers, but all in their own way.

We got to our station at noon and got all our animals out. Poor things, they were just as tired as we were. As soon as they had finished their feed and watering, we got into the saddle again and moved along the roads of Flanders. Oh the mud! It is glorious and such quantities. Why, it is always knee-deep, nobody seems to know. Well, we pushed on in spite of it. What traffic! Horses, mules, motor lorries, motor cars, motor bikes and bikes, and amidst it all the never ending line of infantry. It is simply appalling and yet very few accidents happen. And, as if that were not enough to remind us that a war was still going on, the planes were flitting round in all directions performing the most wonderful glides and dives as if through sheer sport. We kept well to our side and marched in column to the area designated for us. We got there at 5.30pm. Talk of the abomination of desolation!

Such mud. Our horses nearly sank to their bellies, and this is where we were to live! Yes it was true!... You had to whistle. Flanders is bad enough during the winter in peace time, but war makes it one sea of liquid mud. We got back to the road and dismounted, and looked around. Near a hedge we found some petrol tins and we piled these together and threw a wagon cover over and thus made a mess for ourselves.

After our supper, which was a frugal affair, if ever there was one, we looked around us where we were going to pass the night.

There were a few trench boards lying about; these were seized on and made very good beds for weary limbs. Our blanket was soon stretched out and you hadn't to wait long before you found me fast asleep. I believe during the night it poured rain. I believe it, for the authority is trustworthy. But I neither heard nor felt anything. The cover even blew off, I hear, and I was appealed to for assistance, and yet I heard nothing. One thing is certain, next morning, when I awoke, I was quite wet and I had an extra proof for the truth of the statement that it had rained during the night. I poured forth an earnest prayer for having been protected during the night, for Fritz had visited us with his air fowl species, which had deposited a number of those darling eggs, which were by no means golden. Such was our first night in Flanders.

Orders came in immediately after breakfast. Shells, shells and plenty of shells. Horses, mules, men all were busy bringing up the stuff for the guns. The guns were in a nasty position and yet these had to be reached. Our men were lined up. I went round the Catholics to see they were all right. In parts I was up to my knees in the liquid mud. You can't walk, for if you lift your feet – yes, the feet come, but the boots remain behind, so what you do – you wade or slide or, as they say in Ireland, you "slider" through. It was strange, serious, and yet a bit – well, were it not so sacred, I would say comical. There I was between two mules, hearing the men's confessions and then getting behind a timber for another's, out in the road for another, in fact anywhere they wanted me. I got through them all, and order for advance came. I went along the road with them. Then I stood and watched them go forward and gave them a special blessing.

All returned except two, one of whom was a Catholic who however was not seriously wounded. We set to settle a place for ourselves and got under way with shovel, axe, and hammer and soon fixed up the little dug out I spoke about in the beginning. I got round my other sets of men to let them know where they could find me, and see if they wanted to go to confession. Naturally you have no churches or chapels here and you have to make the best of a bad job. You have to go round and find out the Catholics and tell them what to do, where to find you, where there will be Mass, at what time there will be confessions etc. Then the guns themselves had to be visited. I got my steel helmet and gas mask, and with the Blessed Sacrament, which I had consecrated at Mass that morning, in my pyx, next to my heart, I set of on my perilous journey. It was a long dreary trudge, but a real labour of love. The mud and slush was dreadful. But on I went past the naval guns, the siege pieces, the heavies, all roaring and barking away. It is really dreadful when these pieces go off. When you are only a few yards away, it is deafening in real earnest. All put fingers in their ears, and even with that you would imagine at times the drums were burst. Well, on I went and then out into the open along the trench boards until I came upon our guns. I saw the lads, heard their confessions and crept into the little dug-out – an old "pill box" captured from the Bosche. We were all on our knees for we could not stand erect and there, in such surroundings, I gave Holy Communion to these brave lads, for they are brave to stand up in the midst of such danger. There were no flowers or ornamentations of any kind and you fully realised the wonderful love of our Lord for us to come and console us in such conditions as we were placed in.

When we had finished our short thanksgiving, we came out and looked all round. Such guns! Everywhere you looked there was one, and no such thing as cover. Fritz could see our guns, we can see his, and the constant banging is really incredible. How any human beings stand it, I don't know. I had been up among the batteries on our other front, but there it is so to say – reasonable, but up here the numbers are beyond all belief. The shells were dropping all around, and you had to mind yourself, but it is strange how you get accustomed to it all.

The shells burst, and if they are not too near, you don't pay any attention at all. If they happen to approach you, you stand and watch; when they come too near, you lie down just like a dog. I had to go up to the gun position to bury a poor Catholic gunner. Again, we were in the open and under observation. I read the prayers and blessed the grave. A piece of shell fell into the grave beside us. Two more had to be buried then, and their bodies were already there, but no order for burial had been given,

YPRES, BELGIUM
The infantry walking through the mud and desolation

so we went to one of the batteries to find somebody who would give us the necessary details. As we were waiting, Fritz must have thought we were some scouting party, for he began to drop shells around us, and we thought it safer to get under cover and await the return of our messenger. Just as we were getting into one of Fritz's own pill boxes, but which is in our hands now, he dropped a beautiful "dud", and luckily it was a "dud" – only a few yards from us. A "dud", as you know, I suppose, is only a shell that does not explode. Well, when things were quiet, we went back to the grave to bury the poor lads. We had to lower them ourselves.

It was a sight I shan't forget in a hurry. The bodies were wrapped in a blanket, boots, clothes and all, and thus it was we lowered them into a grave, which was half filled with water and liquid mud, and I thought of the 'Roll of Honour' at home. How different from the reality. But what did these poor lads care now? Their souls, I am sure, were already enjoying their well-earned reward. We had lowered them, and during the prayers, Fritz sent about seven shells all round. They were very close, so close we had to lie down and twice we were covered with the shower of thin mud and dust, which the explosions caused. I shan't forget funerals like that in a hurry. It became so hot, we had to leave and told some men to cover them in, when the shelling stopped. That is Fritz. He must have seen what we were doing and it is cruel to think that he would shell us burying the dead. But it is the usual complaint. Dressing stations are shelled, stretcher bearers carrying wounded are shelled and sniped, and worse still he sends gas shells around the advanced aid-posts. That is really cruel, and it is the employment of such methods and tactics as these that has caused Fritz to be despised by all. He is not a "sport". Like today, eleven of his flying machines came across. The anti-air-craft put up a barrage. They managed to turn it. Three of our machines went up and all the Fritzes turned and fled for home. He is not a "sport"! He stands a lot, and is standing a wonderful amount at present, but he is not a sport. Well, we got home safe that day again, though we had to lie down and dodge a few on the way. That is a bit of our work…

My Sunday masses for the men have been said in all kinds of places. Up to the present up here always in the open, for the simple reason there is no place else near. Sometimes I place my altar in a tent, sometimes in a kind of recess made with shell boxes, other times in a corner covered all round with petrol tins. Strange, you will say. Yes, very strange, but we are at war and right in the middle of it. The poor men are delighted, and you should see them, how frequently they assist and receive Holy Communion. Our Catholic officers give very good example in that point and are always the first at their duties. I must say they are all Irish and I am very proud of them. It is a grand example to the men.

During the week I get around the odd units and some days I have great crowds, some who have not seen a priest for I don't know how long... One day last week I said Mass for the British West Indian Regiment. They are great fellows and reminded me very much of my days in Ceylon. They are all coloured of course, but the Colonel is an Englishman and a Catholic and a fine one at that. There he was in the front row. He went to confession and a great number followed his example. They were so glad to be able to assist at Mass, above all said by a Jesuit. It reminded them of home, for the Jesuits have the mission there. I am writing to the Bishop to tell him…

Another part of my work is the visits to the dressing station. Oh, such sights you have here. During the push, I was up during three nights. At home people see the wounded men when they have been through several aid-posts and dressing stations, and they are respectable, for they are bandaged etc. But when you see them brought in directly after a bombing raid or in the middle of the push, it is really frightful. I don't seem to mind it, but a number can't stand it. I go around hear their confessions when there is time, but above all give them absolution and anoint them, and I give conditional (absolution) to the unconscious…

Since I started this letter, I was knocked down with trench fever, a grandiose name for something we know nothing or next to nothing about. You shiver, your teeth chatter, you get high fever, and for days after you feel seedy, very seedy, and then you come round again. It is a strange thing. It is the damp and the cold, but I shall get accustomed to it.

I left my dug-out and am at present in a semi dug-out tent, if you can understand such a thing. It is something like this. The space that would be covered by an ordinary tent is dug up and the soil thrown into a kind of hollow wall made of iron rods and wire netting. This wall is 4ft high and 2ft thick. A block is now placed in the centre of the dug-out space and the ordinary tent pole is placed on that. The ends of the tent are drawn over the top of the patent wall and lo and behold! you have a beautiful dwelling in which you can stand erect at the edge of the tent. My bed is on one side, my table, which serves as altar, on the other. That is not all, we bored a hole through the patent wall and shoved a shell case through to act as a chimney. We built a brick grate with bricks and mud around this and there you have a perfect fireplace. So I am very snug. The door of the tent is well protected for, out in front we have a wall of sand bags and consequently, unless we get a direct hit from a shell or a bomb, I am as safe as can be. I am certainly splinter proof, which is a great point here. We have a few lids of shell boxes on the floor and our feet are dry. What do you think of that? Such comfort, even in Flanders. It is beautiful as long as the wind does not blow the wrong way, for then it is just like a gas attack.

I am as happy as the day is long, the men are fine fellows and the Catholics are tip top, they want an odd pulling up, but it is good in spite of all to see how anxious they are. For there are no such things as churches here, as I said, no houses, no large tents where you can say Mass. You have to fish out places and make the best of a bad job. Then, perhaps, when everything is nicely arranged, orders come in and off they have to go, for the war can't stop till you are ready. Last Sunday I said Mass in a bath house. It was served by a Colonel, who went to communion with a good number of the men. He is a fine fellow. I have only four Catholic officers in the Artillery, but they are really good. We have an American doctor attached now. He is a Catholic too. These Americans are fine fellows. No such thing as human respect about them. The last front I was in, I came across a big number of them and I must say they are [fine] Catholics. Their arrival in France will do an immense amount of good, for people will see that republicanism does not mean French anticlericalism and that a man may be broadminded and be a Catholic at the same time.

The Catholics are showing up really well during the war. "Ah!" said one of the *Gros Bonnets* [bigwigs] lately, "your religion is not like the others." "No of course not," I replied, "sure how could it, seeing ours is the only true one." Our Colonel, a short time ago speaking about Catholics and their religion, said to me: "You know, that is the great difference between your religion and the others, yours has some discipline in it." It is strange, is it not? that it should appeal to men so much, and yet, as I said in my short sermon last Sunday on the mustard seed, talking about the growth of the Church, there are no externals out there to appeal to men. There is no show or band promenades about our religious practices, and yet it is the only religion that has caught men's minds. To men who think, it is the only religion, and how happy would a number be, if, as they say, we would only amalgamate. It is strange, but, as I told them, the secret is because it gets at men's hearts, at men's consciences and doing this, doing it so thoroughly, proves the divinity of its Founder. Such a conglomeration of others: Church of England, Wesleyan, Primitive Methodists, United Board,... and ours purely and simply Catholic. You know, it's grand. And I always tell the men so. Do you know what a Church of England parson told me lately, that he is going to study theology after the war. Well, I wonder, will it be a *biennium* [Two-year course].

Father, enough of this, go on praying for me. I want all the prayers I can get, in order to be able to know what to do and then the strength to do it. That is our chief difficulty here. It all appears so, if I may say so, hodge-podge. You make arrangements and old Fritz knocks everything on the head, and still you go on and do the best you can. But that is the chaplain's work here. Make the best of a bad job in the interest of religion. I need not tell you how delighted I am to get your letters, and your last, as I told you, 'bucked me up,' as the men say. For Fr Proces was afraid you would take it – well not so well. I am delighted, I say, and if I do go to heaven from Flanders, well I shall be able to pray for you all – even with more fervour than I do now, for I never forget you or the Mission in my daily Mass. Remember me to all friends in Galle, a letter to each is impossible, they know that. . . .

In 1918, Fr Delaney, in three letters captured the vicissitudes of war as his contingent was changed over and back from Belgium to France and suffered ignominious retreat before embarking on a relentless final advance.

Belgium, Feb 1918

Dear Fr Superior,

Letter writing and Chaplain's work, though not altogether contradictions in terms, yet are often bordering on that. We are always on the move. Going from camp to camp looking up "auld sinners" and then from camps to the guns, then from one place to another, and even when you would like to drop a few lines, that's just the day you can't get any place to write, or even if you did, you would not be allowed, as all lights have to be put out owing to the visits of those beautiful war productions called "Gothas".

Well, since I wrote to you last, I have been around about a good deal: Belgium, France, Belgium again, then once more sunny France and then back to Belgium once more. We pulled out and went on a long "trek". Such weather! Such roads! Such fields! Even at it's best a "trek" for artillery is always a bit of an upside down kind of affair, but, as they were going for a rest, I went on leave. We get leave, as you know I suppose, every four months or round about that. I got back to Milltown Park and enjoyed the luxury of a bed once more and a clean table cloth, etc. It is a strange life we lead!

Well, when I got back after my fourteen day's leave, I found my men nestling amidst the hills and vales of France. The country was beautiful, really beautiful, and the people were really "charmant". They couldn't do enough for you, and above all for "Monsieur L'aumonier". I was billeted in a very nice farm and "Madame" was really delighted. You should see her talk to the neighbours and tell them that the officer she had was different from all the others, as he was a Catholic Priest. I said Mass in the village church and this created a stir. Even the altar boys with their big eyes and round chubby faces could not refrain from passing quite a large quantity of remarks about my dress and my accent even during Mass. But you should have seen the big broad smile that broke and rippled in continuous waves over those same chubby faces when I put my hand in my pocket and gave them something to buy sweets. Human nature is the same everywhere. Well, it was too good to last, for we were quite happy down there. However, we soon started back for the front. We spent four days on the trek, sleeping in different villages all along the route, meeting with the greatest hospitality everywhere we passed through France. I could say Mass each morning in the village churches, where the *curés* are quite delighted to do anything for you.

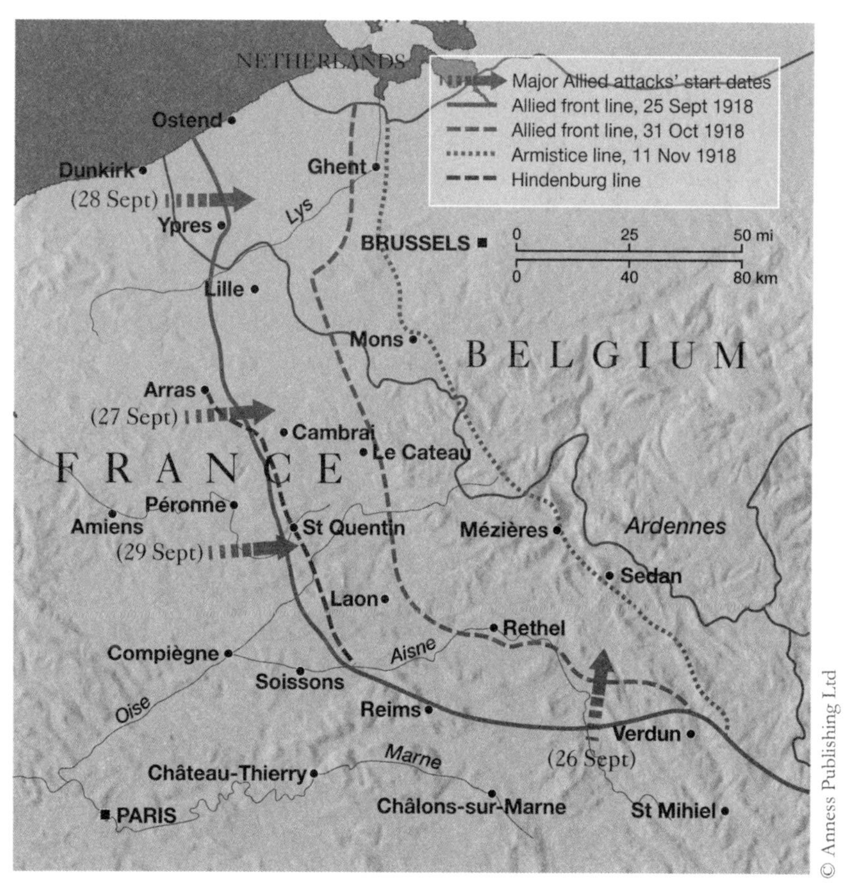

First World War Map

And here we are once more pounding away at old Fritz and he pounding at us. It is strange and both are supposed to be Christians. We have rigged up a little chapel in the – I was going to say village – but to be more exact in the place that was once a village, for churches, houses, everything is smashed and powdered down. It is a sad sight to see so many churches in such an awful state. We have Mass regularly with confessions and communions for the poor lads, who have to suffer so much. In another place we keep the Blessed Sacrament for the communions of men passing by on their way to the front line. It is really consoling to see so many who profit of this great favour of communicating without observing the fast – both officers and men.

Our camp at present is the usual type of all artillery camps – mud – slush – mud! Where it comes from? Whither it all goes? are questions!... well, I at least am unable to answer. My present abode of peace is a regular beauty! The remnant of an old stable wall forms the back. We have run up a few sheets of corrugated iron for the roof and sides and in this "mansion of the blest" sleeps your humble servant, – the sleep of the just. We have piled up heaps of mud, and there is plenty of it here, all around the sides to prevent splinters of shell or bomb from coming in contact with the "*Aumonier militaire*".

The road up to the guns is a dreadful sight! For miles around the country is nothing but one great plain of desolation, mud, slush and mud everywhere, with shell holes in every foot of it, which gives the whole country the appearance of the lid of a huge pepper canister. On all sides lie smashed tanks, broken down wagons, motor lorries, which were shelled and are still. Carcases of horses rotting away in all stages of corruption, meet your gaze at every step. They have tried to bury the men, Germans and British, but it is not finished yet. It is a sad sight and you begin to wonder how it is possible for human beings to advance over a country like that and to live in it when they have advanced.

I was bringing up communion the other day to the guns and I sat down on a heap of stones watching Fritz shell the remnants of a village church. Apart from the awful desecration, it was a glorious sight to see the huge clouds of red dust being sent up into the air and then sail round on the breeze. When he ceased, I pushed on as I thought of the truth of the saying: "One live chaplain is worth 50 dead ones". I got up to the guns all right. It is wonderful all the same how one manages to get through it all, to hear a whizz over your head and then to see a burst just on the spot you were a few moments before, and yet it is not wonderful in the least, when you begin to think of all the prayers offered up for your safety. As I was talking to the Major at the door of the dug-out, whirr! went another over our heads with a bang and a burst. What's that! Strange burst! Is it a dud or a gas shell? Another soon confirmed us and another and yet another to the tune of eighteen! Yes they were gas shells so we disappeared and waited till Fritz would change his mind. He did, and, lo and behold, the net result of eighteen gas shells round and about us – some of which were near enough – was to send us all into our dug-outs to wait and see. It is strange, as I said, and yet not a bit strange. It is all the good prayers that do that for us and we are most thankful for them. They keep us out of harm's way and keep harm out of ours. I got back across that sea of mud, along the duck walks, which are laid down on huge props driven down into the mud. How people can say that Fritz will advance on the Western Front, I can't understand, unless perhaps he intends bringing over his guns in Zepps [Zeppelin – German airship]. I am able to say Mass each morning with a rare – very rare – exception. This in itself is a great consolation amidst all this ruin of every thing sacred. I hope you got my card for X'mas. It was our divisional issue for this year.

Today is Sunday. I said my two Masses, one in a broken down farm and my second in a hut, which is used for a canteen in one of the lines. We are all so scattered, that of course there is no possible chance of all being able to get to Mass, because even if I could get all, there would always be the war, which still goes on and calls out the men at all kinds of hours and times to do all kind of jobs.

I hope all in St Aloysius' are quite well. Remember me to all, to His Lordship and all in the Bishop's House and all in the Mission. I know they don't forget a poor old sinner out here

> on the Western Front, amidst the mud and slush of Flanders. Talking about mud, I was getting back to my camp the other evening when it was pitch dark. Lorries were on the road and naturally I had to give way. In a minute I was down in a filthy ditch. What could I do but smile and they did smile at me when I got in. Was it not the only thing to do? Certainly I enjoyed it, above all the scraping off process.
>
> Don't forget me in your good prayers and holy sacrifices. With kindest regards to Fr Murphy, Fr Lermusieaux, Brothers Verbrugge and Van Goethem and to all whom I know.
>
> Two of our lads were hit by these spittting machines the second day. It is a strange life is it not? But it is dreadful to see so many suffering and suffering – you are really bound to ask yourself sometimes for what? Is it not a dreadful state of affairs to think that in the height of civilisation brains can be utilised only for the destruction of human kind? For it really comes to this and to establish the principle for the victorious side that right is might.

John's next extant letter was not sent until 13 June. Writing from France, he explained what had happened on the Aisne River since he last wrote. He also mentioned that prior to their sojourn at the Aisne they had a 'rough time' defending Perónne, a key town on a hill dominating the Somme river, and had fallen back to join in the defence of Amiens, a communications centre essential to the conjunction of the British and French armies. In the defence of Amiens from 28 March to 5 April, the 2nd Dublin Fusiliers and the 2nd Munsters suffered heavy casualties as they drove back the Germans in fierce hand-to-hand fighting. On 4 April, massed artillery broke the last German attack. Five days later, however, in a different sector, forty-two German divisions broke the British line in the Lys River Offensive, 9–29 April. In Bethune, in the area around Armentières, eight British and two Portugese divisions were shattered. In the critical situation, the Dublins and other sections of the 50th Division were moved in to help stop the advance. As Delaney observed, they had a difficult 21 days holding back the Bosche.

Their subsequent respite on the Aisne River was very welcome. The sense of peace and relaxation, depicted by Delaney, however, was to receive an unexpected and humiliating disturbance.

GERMAN CHARGE
A German charge with fixed bayonets

Friday, 13th June 1918

Dear Fr Superior,

At length the wanderer speaks and sends you a few lines across the ocean. How often have I wished to sit down and have a chat with you all during the most exciting period through which we have been. It was certainly exciting, and I may add a very rough time indeed. But "*a la guerre comme a la guerre*". You will be pleased no doubt to know that I am at present laid up with a bit of a twisted knee, not owing to "enemy action and shell fire" – but to football. We are supposed to be resting at present after our recent exertions, and to add to the amusement and fun we had an Officers' football match. I was invited to play, and got my place in the team as inside right forward. I had facing me a "back" of tremendous proportions. All he had to do was to get himself into motion, and then woe betide the player who even brushed against him. I had come through the last three stunts without a scratch or a bruise, but owing to this match and this particular "back" I had a bit of a twisted knee and a skinned arm. Anyhow we are resting and a rest under a wagon cover will refit me for further operations.

But what about the war? Doubtless you will have read in the papers of the doings of our division, the 50th. We had come down on the Aisne to a very quiet front – as a reward for our work in the other 'stunts', as they are popularly known, as no British troops had been here before. So there were nothing but compliments flying in the air between French and British, in which the civilians also joined. Oh, we were going to have a great and a grand time! We were admired and we admired. We were scattered through the little villages on the Aisne and were led to believe that things were to be very quiet at least for some time. The country being delightful and the people as charming as the countryside to which they belonged, it was going to be a peaceful war front. The village I was quartered in with the artillery was one of the best of all those round about. But I must say almost all were very pretty in spite of all the Boche ravage. Things being peaceful and so quiet, a number of civilians had come back and started little shops which were patronised by all our Tommies, who seem to manage very well even with two words of French. At least they get what they want.

I was staying in the Mayor's house of Glennes, for now that all the papers have been given the whereabouts of the different divisions engaged, there is no further need of throwing that awful veil of secrecy over our movements. The mayor was a good Catholic. His son was a Jesuit. So I need to say no more. He had two daughters, one of whom was a nurse in the neighbouring military hospital, whilst the other was a refugee from the Ardennes and was for the time being living with her papa along with her husband and her daughter. They were all good Catholics. The nurse was a real true *Francaise* and the mainspring of the Catholic life in the village. She was to have been a nun but, owing to the expulsion of religious and all the rest of the beautiful anticlerical laws formed and promulgated by the Republic fighting for "Freedom", she determined to remain in her village. She went in for nursing and got all kinds of diplomas. As there was no doctor in the village, she nursed all the sick and infirm. As there was no *curé* she had to look after the spiritual welfare of the village. Besides, she taught the children their prayers and catechism, prepared them for their first confession and First Communion, had a Children of Mary's sodality for the "grown ups", in fact did everything to keep the Catholic faith fresh and green in the village to which she belonged. In the afternoons she gathered the children of the poorer parents into a kind of work-room, where she taught them sewing etc, and thus enabled the parents to go off and work in the fields. I often thought what an awful pity there are not a few more *Francaises* of that type alive. They would keep poor France still alive, for there is not much religion – at least in the parts of France I visited. Sunday Mass is as much neglected as the week-day Mass. They are baptised; the children make their First Communion, the young people usually get married in the church; and then? – Well, till they die they have no practical relation with the Church and its ministers. It is sad, and many a time I was pained. I may tell you, I often felt sorry also that the division I am attached to is English and consequently on the whole Protestant, – for these poor French can't see the difference, and the fact that all the officers and soldiers don't attend Catholic services is a kind of argument in their favour.

But if there were a few young French women like that nurse, I am more than convinced that things would be otherwise. Naturally then, when I turned up in this village and I was found out to be an SJ, great things were in the air. Grand plans were soon on foot, for the front being so peaceful and all my men being gathered all round the village – a thing not very usual with artillery – everything was favourable. We had Mass every morning and as it was the month of May, we had rosary, benediction and a few "feeling words". We had a real *entente cordiale* service for the feast of St Joan of Arc, and the church was filled with the dull khaki and the bright blue of the Poilus [nickname for French soldiers, like Tommy]. I sang the Mass and preached. Then the nurse gathered all the young *demoiselles* of the district and we had a Children of Mary's meeting on Friday morning, which was the anniversary of one of their companions. We settled them all up and all went to confession and communion. You should have heard me address these young *filles de France* in their mother tongue, but they did not smile, but listened quite attentively. They are really good girls. But I attribute all their goodness after the grace of God to that nurse who devotes her whole life to their spiritual and temporal welfare.

The following Sunday we had a beautiful Requiem for all the officers and men of the 50th division artillery who had fallen during the war. I had had the idea long before, but never had opportunity and, above all, not the materials to give it the splendour it requires; but in this village we had a grand little church – a national monument now – plenty of mortuary drapery in the shape of flags and oriflammes [bright banners] etc, above all most willing hands to help me to decorate it. Strange that the church should be dedicated to St George! Well, that Sunday morning of the 26th May saw the village church of Glennes at its best. Right above the high altar hung a huge black veil with a very large black cross in the middle. We removed all the ornaments from the high altar itself – a point not in complete agreement with the ideas of the mayor's daughter. Then the black drapery ran round the church and the flags and oriflammes hung down the different columns. In the centre of the church we erected a large catafalque, which was covered with a Union Jack, which I had procured from the front-line dressing station. Around about this catafalque stood four of my artillery lads as a guard of honour. They looked really fine as they stood there fully equipped resting on their arms reversed. The officers and men of the French artillery sang the mass for me and I was assisted at the altar by a French soldier priest, who insisted on wearing a black cope. I don't think that the last point was quite rubrical, but we are at war and up at the front, and certainly I think if not permitted it could be tolerated in such circumstances.

After the first gospel I preached, taking as text "greater love than this no man hath etc". The French civilians of the district came in full force. The French officers and soldiers turned in in great numbers to pay a tribute of respect and honour to their allied comrades in arms who had fallen in the good cause. Naturally all our Catholic officers and men were there and proud they were that morning. I need not tell you they looked all they

> felt. But not merely were the Catholics present, the Colonel who is Church of England and a good number of the Protestant officers asked to be allowed to assist. They were much impressed by the service, for a great number had never been to a Catholic service before. Who knows it may be the first step in the right direction for some. God grant it may be so.
>
> You won't be surprised then if I tell you that the mayor's family were radiant with delight. They felt all their troubles, all their hard work had been amply repaid by the success – if I may use such a word – of the Requiem. But things were going to develop as Corpus Christi was the following Sunday. We had already discussed it and had settled on a procession through the village. It was going to be some thing. I had invited the General and Catholic officers of one of our infantry brigades. All was arranged. They were coming over in cars the following Sunday. But alas! man proposes God disposes. I had said several times already that things were too good to last. It was more like peace again. The "Old Boy" himself must have been very angry that religion was beginning to flourish again once more, for on that Sunday night the big attack on the Aisne began.

From harmony to chaotic retreat

General von Ludendorff, having failed to penetrate the northern sector of the British front, turned his attention against the French line on the Aisne River in May 1918. He broke through the line, with devastating effect for Delaney and his men. The German advance reached as far as the Marne before it was halted by a combination of British and American forces at the battle of Château Thierry. It was to prove a turning point. But to return to Delaney's letter and his reaction to the unexpected attack:

> I shan't forget it in a hurry and certainly our poor decimated division will remember it for many a day after this terrible war. We were drenched with gas that night, practically the whole night long. I was up for most of it. Now, it is bad enough for us to suffer this dreadful pest of war, but when the poor civilians have to go through it, above all women and children, it is really dreadful.

Naturally, they all congregated round our quarters for they feel a certain sense of security – though it should be the opposite for where the military are they are sure to have shells and gas – when they are near us. The shelling was dreadful and, as shell after shell burst, the fears of all were increased. It was a dreadful night that. The following morning as I said Mass in the little church, I thought the whole place would be about my ears several times, for the shells kept bursting and pitching about. Houses were being smashed in, dumps were being sent up, and all traffic had to cease as old Fritz was putting plenty of heavy stuff all along the roads. Things did look bad! The wounded began pouring in; we fixed up a kind of dressing station for them where they were treated and had their wounds dressed. But still the shells came on and several were killed. I shall never forget the two poor girls that were hit in their house almost opposite the church. They had run in for safety and whilst in, a huge "heavy" burst on the house and smashed everything in. I anointed both and absolved them. Strange, the younger of the two, aged about nineteen, though far more hit than her sister about twenty-eight, lived the longer. You should have heard her pray with me, poor thing. However, I thought if I could manage to get her to hospital her life might be saved if her leg and arm were amputated. But none of the French ambulances would stop or turn back. So I went to the hospital myself and brought up a horse ambulance. I carried the poor girl in my arms and put her on the floor of the ambulance. But when we got to the hospital all had cleared out, for the Germans were pushing and pushing hard.

They had broken through the French line on our left and had taken our lads by surprise from behind. So we were caught between two fires. Our lads fought and fought well but naturally had to retire, a point which became more evident as soon as it was perceived with what numbers the enemy was attacking. We got a few more wounded settled up and I remained on in the village with the Sergeant Major who was to look after some wagons on which were placed stores etc. But when the German cavalry got into the end of the village, I thought it was time to move.

© The Father Browne Collection

FLANDERS
Gun and artillary at Passchendaele

I moved off with the infantry, but then came military police dashing up to say that the Boche were on our heels. So as a French motor car passed, I held on to the hood and did the giant stride along the road till I managed to swing myself on to the step – for this car could not stop. I got into the next village in this fashion and there I met one of our orderlies, who had another horse besides the one he was riding. So I got on this and managed to get off leaving the Boche far away, but coming on in droves and very fast. The shells kept pouring in and all along the roads men and animals were being knocked out, for Fritz knew the country to a nicety and consequently was well aware of the route of retreat. It was a hot day, I assure you, but I must say, thanks to the good and pious prayers that are offered up for me I managed to get off without even a scratch, though there were some very tight corners. But I lost absolutely all my kit, my altar, my tunic, clothes, breviary – absolutely everything. All I have now is what I was wearing when I got off – a novel way of practising detachment *n'est-ce-pas?*

We got the Mayor and his daughters away in our wagons. I don't know how they got on afterwards, for we were retreating and retreating as long as old Fritz pushed. He did pester us with shells and machine gun fire from his planes. Two of our lads were hit by these fire-spitting machines the second day. It is a strange life is it not but it is dreadful to see so many suffering and suffering – you are really bound to ask yourself sometimes, for what! It is a dreadful state of affairs to think that in the height of civilisation brains can be utilised only for the destruction of human kind, for it really comes to this, and to establish the principle for the victorious side that right is might. It's sad. The sights seen make you think and certainly for me the saddest sight of all is that of the poor refugees fleeing before the enemy. They know what they got in 1914. They don't wish to have a repetition. It is sad. Poor women and children standing along the roads carrying bundles in which they have tied up their few belongings. Yet these French peasants bear it so well. They seem to get so stoical, that it really surprises you when you consider the high sentimentality of the race.

Well, we are on the move still. We suffered heavily and very heavily indeed but strange to say, no Catholic officer got knocked out except an American doctor – a Jesuit boy who was wounded. He was a fine type. When he saw me in the village he offered me his horse and was ready to risk his own life to save mine. The poor fellow had only left me three minutes when the shell burst beside him and wounded him badly. He is at present in a London hospital. During the retreat we slept anywhere and everywhere. We were up at all hours travelling by night and by day always eluding the Boche and fighting our way back to new positions. When we got far back enough, we reformed and fitted one artillery brigade out of the two to go up the line again. I was going back with this new artillery brigade when we got orders again to retire. So the will had to be taken for the deed. At present I am living in an orchard with a wagon cover overhead to protect us from the rain and sun – a necessity for the sun is very strong at present and the rain – well it came down in torrents the other night and I was completely drenched, a little change in the monotony of life!!

Well, that is what happened to us more or less on the Aisne. Before that we had been in the country of Bethune and Armèntieres for twenty-one days holding up the Boche there, when the Portugese gave way. We had a very hot time of it there also, and before that we had been down on the Somme right in front of Perónne and had fought our way back to Amiens, where we succeeded at last in holding up the Boches. That also was a trying time, a rough time. But we had come through without leaving a single man or gun in enemy hands. I suppose we were getting too proud. The last "stunt" has sobered us, for as I said, we lost and lost heavily.

Well, all this has been about myself. How are all in Galle and St Aloysius'? *The Aloysian* is now in Boche hands, as it was in my bag. So that brings the war a little nearer home and makes it more personal. I really don't know when I wrote you last, for I have lost everything and can hardly remember the days or dates, but I think I wrote to you after the Amiens affair.

Well, dear Father Superior, remember me to all the Fathers of Galle. Things look very bright now again and I am sure Bro Polydore smiles as of yore. What about his band? Have they the same tune still or have they started another on account of a war being on? I suppose I shan't be able to recognise the place when I get back with all the improvements already made and others in contemplation. I hope the boys are doing well and that Fr Murphy has a few chances this year in the exams. What about the cricket and football teams? Both doing well, I am sure, as also the cadets.

Good-bye again dear Fr Superior, with renewed good wishes to all the Fathers in Galle and to all my old friends.

By October matters had changed considerably. When he wrote from France on 2nd October 1918, the allied troops were advancing steadily and the end was in sight.

France, Oct 2nd, 1918

Dear Fr Superior,

Thanks very much for your ever welcome and always charming letters. It does one good out here on the plains of death, I may say, to get a few lines from old friends, and from such old friends as are those in our dear old Ceylon. Yes, indeed, Father I often think of you and of you all. Many a time my thoughts wander across the thousands of miles that separate us, and in an instant I am away from all the gunning and killing and slaughter and away back in peaceful Galle. I am not tired of it yet, for though everything about you tends to feed one up, as the men say, owing to all your good and pious prayers, I am in the best of form. Never had better health and though some say I got thin, that does not make much difference provided the health is good.

I always wish to write you a long letter. Hence the hiatus in my correspondence. You got my last letter, I trust, in which I gave you a few details of our affair in May. Our division was mentioned in a special manner, and I know that was a reason for redoubling your prayers for an auld sinner out in France. Yes, we had a rough time of it. I lost absolutely everything, even my vow crucifix, which I had carried through all and which I cherished above all. It was a narrow shave for me, that famous 26th of May. But I did get away absolutely unwounded. Just a few sods of mud and gravel thrown over me by the bursting of shells. That was all. Several times old Fritz came down very close and machine-gunned us from his planes, but again I was safe. So you see the effect – real effect – of your prayers.

Now things are different. We are giving it to Jerry now and I may add he is getting it badly in the neck. We have been through the different advances as we were through the retreats. It is a little different, I may tell you, and though soldiers are not supposed to possess such a thing as sentimentality, advancing has a wonderful influence even on them. Yes, Father, it is easy to fight when things go well. *The Imitation* [*of Christ*] has something to say on the same point and it is perfectly true. The poor French are wonderfully "lucked" – as the men put it – at present. They had dark days as well as ourselves and they rejoice all the more now that things are swinging round.

What a life! What a country! Living anywhere and everywhere. Marching at night; during the day sleeping when and where you get the chance and yet living through it all and, I may say, living well. I have been through the big battles of the Somme and in the advance on Perónne. It was glorious, I need not tell you. Such a number of unwounded prisoners surrendered. Just before one of the big battles, I got into a broken-down village. With the willing assistance of my Catholic lads, we cleared up the church, which had suffered from shellfire. We made it look neat and even prim with the few artificial flowers we found, for we straightened them out and put them on the altar. I had fixed up my notice that there would be Mass at such an hour and confessions and communion. I went up the line to settle my other lads up for I intended saying my second Mass up there. On my return I found a new notice posted on the door of the church about Australians. I had a look in and found one of these fine lads working at the altar.

I had a chat with him and found there was a chaplain who had come in during the night with the troops. I made my way around the shattered houses and found him in one, seated on his blankets in the corner of what was once a cosy little room. We had a chat and fixed up about the morrow, for it was Sunday. I was to say my first Mass in the battered village and go up the line for my second. He was to say the Mass in the village. "What about a combined Benediction in the evening?" I suggested. Right you are! Great! was the immediate reply! On my return from the line the next day what was my surprise to find on the church door a huge poster announcing "A Mission to be preached by the Rev. John Delaney SJ, CF 50th division." It was rather sudden, I assure you. I got off my horse and was reading all details when up came the chaplain who, in his usual smiling way, said: "I knew you wouldn't mind. Besides you Jesuits are always ready for everything". Well – I thought, yes – but – still – anyhow we'll do our best. "I have posted up notices all round, the canteens as well, so you will have a crowded house", he continued.

The front was tolerably quiet, as we were getting ready for the new battle. The officers, all of whom are Protestants, came to me and said: "What time is your service, Father?" – "7pm" I replied. "Will you have any objection to our coming?" they asked. "Oh, you won't get a seat tonight, for the Australians are coming this evening, so there is no use in you turning up". "Well we'll be there, Father", they all shouted in chorus. I went up to the shell-battered church. It was almost half full already. The Australian Chaplain and myself started the confessions and we were going hard for three quarters of an hour. There were no scruples there. So we went hard at it. At 7.00pm we got one of the officers to start the Rosary in order to get as many confessions as possible. We continued hearing. At 7.20pm we stopped. I turned around. The church was packed to the door, gallery and all. We got the altar steps filled as well. It was really a most consoling sight. Down in the church I saw my Protestant friends. We started with the hymn: "Hail Queen of Heaven". These lads did sing. There Australians, Americans and my own artillery lads all blending their voices in the beautiful hymn. I preached on the necessity of the Blessed Eucharist for soldiers. You should have seen them. How they listened, Protestants and all. It was most edifying. At the end of the sermon we had another hymn: "To Jesus Heart all burning", then Benediction after which we gave communion. We had 600 that day. We wound up with the famous hymn: "Faith of Our Fathers". I thought the church would come down. It was really glorious!! We continued our mission as long as we could.

The battle started and all we had was three days, but the attendance was great. The church was full each evening. The second evening, we had 300 communions and the last evening we had 500. So you see your prayers are being heard. The poor lads were in the fray the next morning, but they were all well prepared with "the Bread of the Strong" to meet all emergencies. These Australian lads are great Catholics. There is no human respect about them. They are all straightforward and honest. They don't care about anybody and woe betide the man that says anything against the Catholics. I am not surprised that the Boche fear them. I need not tell you all the Protestant officers were greatly impressed by the whole service as they call it. There

© The Father Browne Collection

NO MAN'S LAND

was no force employed. They had come purely and chiefly of their own free will. "We can't understand it", said one at dinner, "how the Catholics are so attached to their religion". "Oh, quite easy is the answer", I replied smiling. "It is simply a question of faith appealing to intelligence".

The advance came off all right. In fact I should have been surprised had it not, for there is such stuff in these Australians that nothing can stop them. The whole area was packed with artillery and when all the guns, heavies as well as field, began to speak, it was simply marvellous. If you could only forget the consequences it would be really theatrical.

Then again the preparations were so enormous. We were run into the area again and started piling up stuff almost immediately. Shells, shells and more shells had to be got up to the guns. Then forward positions had to be selected and these places packed with shells so that the guns, when they would go forward, could have everything ready to poop off. This was the dangerous work for it had to be done at night and naturally Fritz kept all the roads under shell fire. I was up with the party and how men manage to live through it and come through without even a scratch is a marvel. One of my Catholic lads had three horses killed under him. Another of our sergeants had his horse wounded in seventeen places another night, and yet he was untouched. Well, things went on gaily and the stuff was piled up. Tanks were moving forward sometimes 150 a night. That was some noise as the Yanks say. Crushing and crushing all before them and then halting anywhere they could get a bit of a hedge. It was astonishing, walking about the line the day before the attack came off, to find tanks everywhere and yet old Fritz never suspected it. The heavy guns were mingled with the field and thus did not give the show away. Things did look blue at one moment for he made an attack and blew up some ammunition which we had stacked and even captured prisoners. But he didn't go far enough. The day previous to the advance, I was all around the guns and saw my lads.

It was really glorious. Enthusiasm was in the air. The guns were polished and well oiled: everything was ready. "Yes, Father, a great number of old scores have to be settled tomorrow". "Yes, we are going to get some of our own back". "Yes, indeed, time for him to get some of what he gave to us and he is going to get it". Officers and men were in great form. Photographs of the country over which they were to advance had now been taken and were being passed round. All knew where they were to go and what they had to do. The morning dawned and everything went off to the second. The guns started from their new positions and this alone must have "put the wind up Jerry" as the men put it. Tanks crawled along and to prevent the noise, heaps and heaps of straw had been placed all along the roads to deaden the sound. A huge number of planes flew low and buzzed away to still deaden the noise of the tanks so that Fritz would take it to be an air raid pure and simple. The infantry started and over the bogs they went. I was with the infantry that day as they were a chaplain short; so I took his place. It was most exciting and, strange to say, very few casualties on the whole. The German machine-guns did damage of course but the guns were either silenced or captured, and those that did not meet with either fate had to clear. So we had all the excitement and fun – if I might use such a word – of war, without its dangers.

Prisoners poured in, for they were surrendering in thousands. It was grand! We had had to wait for a long time for this day but it came. The tide had turned and it is flowing away still, for the advance is continuing and please God will continue till the whole affair is ended. Thank God, there are great signs of the enemy breaking and if only things can go the way they are going, the end is in sight. You can easily understand our feelings when we began to advance over the same ground we had been forced to leave in March. How everything, even a broken wall, became a point of interest. German sign-boards were up now and every stone, you might say, could tell a tale. It is a strange feeling to come across points that your own men have been firing in for some time and to see that the Germans had been defending them. We had many such points of interest. The advance continued and is still continuing. We are in the midst of it all.

One item more which will interest you. The day before the feast of our Holy Founder [St Ignatius Loyola, 31 July], we halted away out in the middle of the fields. No church anywhere near. So I couldn't let the day go by without some celebration. We fixed on Mass in the open. An altar was fixed up with the blue vault of heaven as cover. An artillery wagon with a piano on it formed our organ-loft. Captain Meagher, my ever-faithful officer, served the Mass. I preached to the men who were all around me in the middle of a corn-field about the qualities of the soldier Saint Ignatius of Loyola. It was a grand sight and I knew that you for one would have been proud and happy to witness such a scene. Well, dear Father, continue your good prayers and get others to pray and pray hard. We have some stiff fighting still before us and as we intend pushing on, it is to be a strenuous time for all. Please God we shall all come through. Remember me to His Lordship, to all the Fathers of the Mission and to the whole community of St Aloysius', not forgetting the lads at the College and all my old friends of Galle.

> Look out for great things in your dear Belgium. It will be stiff work but I think the Allies will do it all right, for all the prayers are going to have their effect. Goodbye for the present.

Delaney's hopes were borne out. With dwindling reserves compared to the Allies, the Germans were given no respite in a series of battles. Using heavy barrages, as Delaney described, and spearheaded by tanks, the allied armies repeatedly broke into the enemy front and out flanked the Germans. Amiens was retaken on 8 August, the Australians crossed the Somme at the battle of Sainte Quentin on 31 August and Perónne was re-entered on 1 September. In these activities the 50th Division, including the Dublin Fusiliers, was active.

Two days after John Delaney's letter, on 4 October, his division participated in the battle of Le Catelet. The fighting, as in all the battles, was fierce. The town was captured on 4 October, retaken by the Germans, and then won back after close quarter fighting. The battle for Le Cateau was waged on 16–17 October. Victory was gained despite intense opposition. H.A. Curtis, of 2nd Dublin Fusiliers, earned the Victoria Cross. At Fontáine Aux Bois, Landrecies, on 4 November, severe casualties were suffered, and John Delaney merited the Military Cross. The war drew to a close at the Forêt de Mormal from 5–7 November. The fighting was intense as the British, including the 50th Division and the 2nd Dublins, sought to force the passage of the Sambre and Oise Canal and to secure a foothold in the Forêt de Mormal, one of the largest forests in France.

On that front on 11 November, it was announced that hostilities were to cease at 11.00am. German machine gun fire, nevertheless, continued all morning until three minutes before eleven when it ceased. But, bizarrely, at two minutes to the hour, a machine gun fired off a complete belt without pause. Then, a single machine-gunner was seen to stand up, take off his helmet, bow, turn, and walk slowly to the rear. Then all was silence.[10]

The Aloysian finished its account on Fr Delaney by rejoicing on his gaining the Military Cross:

> Old Aloysians will be glad to hear that the Reverend Father John J. Delaney SJ of St Aloysius' College, Galle, has been awarded the Military Cross for conspicuous bravery and devotion to duty

John Delaney SJ recieved the Military Cross, but in the photograph, right, is the British War Medal and the Victory Medal, both of which he also received

© Irish Jesuit Archives

during the war and in particular in the October offensive, when he accompanied his battalion throughout the campaign which terminated in the victory of the British troops at Fontaine-aux-Bois, near Landrecies, France, on 4th November, a few days before the armistice was signed. Rev. Father Delaney is still ministering, as a military Chaplain, in the 2nd Battalion, Royal Dublin Fusiliers, 50th Division BEF. We offer our congratulations to the Reverend Father who, we understand, is to rejoin the staff of St Aloysius' College next year.

John Delaney's cheerful and unassuming account of his activities gives little indication of his impact on officers and men. A report on him, however, in the papers of the senior Catholic chaplain in France, Fr B.S. Rawlinson, OSB, paints a very vivid picture.[11] The report's glowing appreciation of his conduct as military chaplain indicates that he virtually emulated Fr Doyle in his interest in the men, in his daring activities to bring sacramental absolution and comfort to the wounded and the dying, and in his cheerfulness of spirit in the most adverse situations. The report also indicated that his chaplaincy had been changed to the artillery attached to the 2nd Division of the Royal Dublin Fusiliers. It also attributes his Military Cross to his bravery at the battle of Le Cateau rather than at Fontaine-aux-Boix, though his outstanding service in both locations is praised and acknowledged.

The Report on his chaplaincy

FATHER JOHN DELANEY

Fr Delaney acted as chaplain for just two years, from August 18th 1917 to 2nd September 1919, but, short as the time was, it was full of very active life. The many places in which he served read like a geography lesson – Arras, Perónne, Somme, Le Catelet, Fôret de Mormal, Landrecies – and his splendid record, not only in distinctions but in the high and affectionate esteem of officers and men, shows that in him they saw always the priest who had one cause at heart – their spiritual welfare. His great natural gifts – a character brimming over with sunshine and good nature, musical talents and an untiring power of work – went far of course to win for him the fragrant memories that he has left in the 50th Division.

Lieut Colonel K.C. Weldon CO 2nd Batt Royal Dublin Fusiliers writes of him:

> *He was with me from September 1918 till June 1919. He greatly distinguished himself by his fearless conduct under fire, especially in the big fight at Le Cateau, October 1918, when he won the Military Cross. Even when the Battalion came out of fight, he spent days afterwards searching for the missing under heavy shell fire, and was rewarded by finding and burying all our dead. He took the greatest interest in the men, and the fact that there was practically no crime and such a good tone in the Battalion, I put down entirely to his individual care and interest in the men. He was indefatigable too in arranging sports and concerts to amuse them during the dreary time spent in bad billets after the armistice. I can honestly say that of all the good priests I had the honour to serve with in various Battalions, Father Delaney was the best. He has been a great loss to us and we miss his kindly word and cheery smile.*

One can easily understand that a chaplain with this record had no difficulty about arranging services for his men. "You, Father, can have service here always. You do something for the men. They are the better after it. Your religion has discipline."

One evening on the Somme, the officers were discussing about a very large voluntary service of Australians and Dublins, just held. "What is it you do to the men", asked the Commanding Officer of Fr Delaney. "What is it you have that grips them?" "I can tell you, sir," interposed an officer. "The RC chaplain is to the men what the men call him, Father. That is the whole secret." Asking for lorries to take the men to midnight Mass in Flanders, he was told by a Staff Captain: "Yes, Father, anything you want, lorries, cars, I know you use them and we reap the benefit." On this occasion the whole regiment, officers and men, were present with [the] band, and all Catholics went to Holy Communion. A choir of 40 sang the Mass, trained by Fr Delaney; and a Guard of Honour of 21 were in the Sanctuary.

On the Feast Day of the Church in their district in France the Australians joined the Dublins in the procession, the officers carrying banners. The French people were wild with joy. The local paper next day wrote: "Honour to those who combine patriotism with religion. When will it be allowed to our own soldiers to pay the same honour to their God in their own country as we saw last evening in the case of the brave soldiers of our gallant Allies?"

A Dublin Fusilier, NCO, writing about Fr Delaney says: "The one we love in our regiment is our priest. We know he came out here for us and he is always with us and is always there where he is wanted. Could we do otherwise than love such a one? That's the reason we worship the ground he walks on."

An Anglican officer attached to Dublin Fusiliers, who had been preparing for the ministry before joining up, took part in the last prayers conducted by Fr Delaney before they went over the ridge in October 1918 at Le Cateau. A machine gun riddled him with bullets before he had gone twenty yards. Fr Delaney buried him with the others and had a letter from his father, a clergyman in England, enclosing an extract from the last letter of his son:

> *We've had no service of our own today. I went to the Roman Catholic service. But my! Its wonderful how these Catholics cling to their religion. It does mean something to them, and look what it does for them. And the life we are living out here seems to make them more devoted to it. They are the finest set of fellows I ever came across, and*

better still, the cleanest living men that I ever mixed with or lived amongst.

Testimony such as this is surely high praise, alike to the men themselves and to the chaplain who was so long in charge of them. In spite of being exposed to the gravest danger many times from shell and rifle fire, Fr Delaney was laid up twice only with trench fever.[12] An extract from 50th Div GRD December 21 1918 reads:

> *At Fontaine aux Bois, November 4th 1918, several casualties occurred. Fr Delaney immediately collected stretcher bearers and had the wounded removed to an adjacent cellar, remaining in the barrage himself comforting the wounded till all had been received. In the absence of a Medical Officer, he organised a First Aid Station, and attended to the wounded, thereby undoubtedly saving many lives. During the engagement he was ever present where casualties were heaviest. His conspicuous bravery and disregard for personal safety in dressing and remaining with the badly wounded in the open was beyond praise.*

Hence one is not surprised in reading that the men were especially pleased to hear the Major General commanding 50th Division saying to Fr Delaney, as he presented him with the ribbon of the Military Cross, "I always consider it an honour and a privilege to be able to confer a decoration on a chaplain of your denomination."

In addition to this decoration Fr Delaney was mentioned in despatches and recommended for DSO. He can count on the hearty good wishes of the many he helped in his arduous mission work in far away Ceylon.

From decoration to demobilisation and renewal

The remarks of the reporting officer on 2 January 1919, relating to Delaney and the conferring of the Military Cross, were brief and unadorned:

> Captain the Revd J. Delaney has given the greatest moral support and assistance to the officers commanding the battalion to which he has been attached, both in action and in billets. He has

> identified himself with the men and taken the keenest interest in their comfort and welfare. He has given the greatest assistance in the carrying out of the education scheme, and has proved himself to possess valuable organising powers in this connection.[13]

The words 'he has identified himself with the men' was doubtless made easier by Delaney's own working class background.

John Delaney was demobilised on 14 June 1919. He returned to England with a small group of his unit on 23 June, reporting to Colchester and finally to Aldershot.[14]

He had been through a life-changing experience. He would miss the friendship and comradeship formed in the intensity of war, but he had other memories that would disturb his sleep: memories of trench war, of the big bombardments before attack, of Flander's mud, and of the compassion that seized him as he 'peered at the doomed and haggard faces of the men.'[15]

After a couple of months back in Ireland, John went to the Jesuit house at Tullabeg, near Tullamore, in the Midlands. There he entered on his tertianship – a year of spiritual renewal for Jesuits, undertaken frequently by priests after ordination and the completion of theological studies. Delaney, after two years in the noise and turmoil of war, probably felt the need for spiritual renewal and the quiet rural surroundings provided by Tullabeg. With his very active temperament, however, it is not unlikely that, as the months passed, the quiet routine of his life proved taxing. By the end of the nine or so months of the tertianship, it may be hoped that, despite the psychological scars of war, John was rested physically and enlivened spiritually as he prepared to return to Ceylon. He returned as the prefect of studies, or headmaster, of the familiar St Aloysius College, Galle.

NOTES

1. Rawlinson Papers, Downside Abbey Archives, courtesy Stephen Bellis, who has generously made available the information on John Delaney that he came across in the Downside Archives and the British Public Records Office.
2. National Archives. Public Record Office. War Office. 374/19114
3. Idem.
4. Idem.
5. Delaney-Provincial, T.V. Nolan, Tuesday, no date, Irish Jesuit Archives (IJA), J 29 CH P 1/12 (1)

6. Idem, 23 Sept. CH P I/12 (2)
7. Fr Gleeson was one of the best known of the Irish chaplains and features in a celebrated painting on horse back blessing the massed ranks of Irish troops.
8. IJA. 6 Dec 1917, J 29 CH P I/12 (3)
9. The poem entitled 'To My Darling Daughter Betty' includes the lines:

You'll ask why I abandoned you, my own,
And the dear heart that was your baby throne,
To dice with death. And Oh! They'll give you rhyme
And reason: some will call the thing sublime,
And some decry it in a knowing tone.

So here, while the mad guns curse overhead,
And tired men sigh with mud for couch and floor,
Know that we fools, now with the foolish dead,
Died not for flag, nor King, nor Emperor,
But for a dream, born in a herdsmen shed,
And for the secret Scripture of the poor.

10. Col H.C. Wylly. *Crown and Company (2nd Bat Royal Dublin Fusiliers)*, vol 2, p. 121, cit Tom Johnstone. *Orange Green and Khaki (the story of the Irish regiments in the Great War, 1914–18)*, Dublin 1992, p. 424. Much of my information on the battles is drawn from *Orange, Green and Khaki.*
11. Rawlinson Papers, box Ephemera, 103-0085/0092
12. Trench Fever was contacted from the ever present lice and was one of the most frequent ailments among troops in the First World War. It was marked by severe headaches, pains in joints, and such effects as depression, weakness, and insomnia. It lasted 5–6 days, but often recurred.
13. National Archives PRO, WO 514/19114. The words of the Reporting Officer were signed by Brigadier General Robinson (this name is difficult to read).
14. Idem.
15. Siegfried Sassoon. 'Aftermath' in *Poetry of the First World War*, ed Marcus Clapham, (The Collector's Library: London, 1913).

Chapter 4

FINAL YEARS ON TWO CONTINENTS

Ceylon: Headmaster to Preacher, 1921–1931

Setting the scene

The impact of the World War in Ceylon and elsewhere was to increase the sense of national identity and the desire for greater political representation. At the Annual General Meeting of the Catholic Union of Ceylon, on 15 October 1922, Fr S.G. Perera SJ, a colleague of Delaney who had lived in Ceylon for many years, delivered a lecture on 'Catholics and Nationalism'. He spoke of the mixture of many races and religions in Ceylon and of the general spirit of tolerance among them. He noted, however, the presence of an extreme minority among the Buddhists who sought the exclusion of all Western religions in the name of the national purity of the Sinhalese people, their culture and national identity. Significantly, despite his reference to a general spirit of tolerance, Perera urged Catholics to use Catholic social teaching as their own, not that of the Church, and to seek the overall national welfare, fostering harmony between races and religion.[1]

On the political front, meantime, a Ceylon National Congress had been formed which sought to achieve such harmony. It aimed to be representative of all political and racial groupings in the island. The endeavour was undermined by Sinhalese extremists, similar perhaps to those mentioned by Perera, who took over the congress. As a result, when John Delaney returned to Ceylon at the start of the 1920s, the politics of the island was already beginning to be polarised into two feuding groups – the Sinhalese, represented by the Ceylon National Congress, and the Tamils.

More immediately relevant to his situation, however, is, perhaps, the depiction of Ceylon presented at the Apostolic School, Mungret College, in 1926. It told of the Ceylon mission, its peoples, and the condition of education in the island. The speaker, Fr Tim Long, worked in Ceylon but currently was studying at Cambridge University. The country, Long explained, was roughly three-fourths the size of Ireland, with a similarly sized population of four and a half million. There were two main races in the island, the Tamils in the North and the numerically stronger Sinhalese in the South. Their languages were quite different. In addition, there were Mahommedans, and the descendants of Europeans, mainly of Dutch and Portuguese descent. There were also, of course, Europeans employed by the British administration or otherwise working in Ceylon as businessmen, teachers, missioners. In Fr Long's view, Ceylon was 'the best organised foreign mission in the Church today'. He praised its bishops, priests, religious sisters and brothers, for their work, and commented that 'as a consequence, the Catholic Church today' was 'undoubtedly the greatest educational factor in the island'. Catholics held 'some of the highest state appointments' and commanded 'a reputation for integrity far beyond that of any other persuasion'.[2]

Headmaster at St Aloysius

Allowing for some over-statement in this account, John Delaney, on his return, found the Catholic Church in an assertive position. He himself was headmaster of a magnificent new college, situated on an eminence entitled Mount Calvary, with St Mary's Catholic Cathedral on one side and the convent of the Sacred Heart Sisters on the other. The new College of St Aloysius housed over 500 boys. His predecessor, Fr Murphy, moreover, had developed a remarkable spirit of work among the students, who, it is said, greatly revered him for his kindness, simplicity, and discernment.[3]

Unfortunately, efforts to glean information about Fr John Delaney's

MISSIONERS IN GALLE, CEYLON
Rev. C. Pilar SJ (1897-1901); Fr D. Murphy SJ; Rev. J. Delaney SJ (1899-1904)

time as headmaster have not been successful. Since 1971, the school has been taken over by the Sri Lanka government and caters almost entirely for Buddhist pupils. The list of past headmasters shown on the college's website has Delaney occupying the position from 1921–1925. Given his energy, power of organisation and cheerful disposition, and his previous happy experience of the college, a longer spell as headmaster might have been expected. Why he lasted only four years is not clear. Perhaps he was no longer adaptable to school life? It is always difficult to follow a greatly loved and successful headmaster, and army experience is not always a good preparation for dealing with teachers and schoolboys. Many military chaplains, used to working with and for men in conditions of life and death, have found it difficult to settle into the daily routine of school life, let alone guiding and directing a large school. On the other hand, in the light of previous experience, was his short term as principal the result of a revival of the Belgian Fathers unhappiness with the 'English' form of education? National identity in various forms took on new life after the First World War, and Bishop Van Reeth, the occasion of Delaney's presence in Ceylon, had died in 1923. His insistence on having native English speakers in a school that taught subjects through English, and preferably being in charge of the school, appears to have ended shortly after his death. From 1925 onwards, the headmasters were Belgian Jesuits. Delaney was succeeded in 1925 by Ernest Gaspard SJ, who continued in office until 1949. In the event, John Delaney, in 1925, was entrusted with a task related to the long established St Mary's College, and St Mary's Church, at Kegalle in the centre of the island.[4]

The Aloysian, in its 1956–57 issue, following John Delaney's death, reported that:

> ...the urgent need of a capable Head for the promising school at Kegalle directed the attention of the Superiors to Father Delaney as the best man for the responsible post. He was transferred to his new field at the beginning of 1925 and remained there and did solid work till 1932. The new St Mary's College, a stately building, easily the best of the district, was the result of his energetic enterprise.[5]

From school to pulpit

Very little has been learned about John's time at Kegalle. Such second hand reports as are available, suggest that within a few years his time and effort were devoted to the pastoral activity offered by St Mary's Church. The *Mungret Missionary Magazine,* 1929, mentioned that it had learned from Ceylon that Fr John Delaney was no longer engaged in school work. It surmised that the St Aloysius College was the poorer, 'and the little church at Kegalle the richer'.[6] Three years later, the *Mungret Annual,* July 1932, reported that Delaney was 'easily the most popular and effective preacher in the island, a wonderful raconteur, and doing no end of good'. By that date, however, John Delaney had already returned to Ireland. *The Aloysian,* in the issue mentioned, observed that:

> ...while in Kegalle, or as was thought, during a short stay at Trincomalee where he had gone for ministry, Fr Delaney fell a victim to acute malaria which did not yield to any remedy. His constitution became so badly affected that the doctors ordered him home as the only hope of a cure. He left in 1932, never to return to the land and the work he loved so much.

MUNGRET ANNUALS

He retained, however, a keen interest in Galle and Ceylon into his final years. Anyone coming from there was besieged with questions about old friends and pupils, how the school was progressing academically and in games. He looked forward to receiving *The Aloysian* every year until shortly before his death.[7]

The return home

Blest with great energy, John Delaney was always occupied with one activity or another. All the indications are that he was a workaholic. This was borne out by the report in the *Mungret Annual* in August 1933:

> Fr J.J. Delaney SJ, is home from Kegalle, Ceylon. It was said that he came home for a rest. Fr John's definition of a rest must be the change of climate, for he has never ceased work once he returned. He has made a name in Ireland already as a preacher and director of retreats. On Whit Sunday he received our sodalists[8] and delighted all the boys with his sermon for the occasion. We have seldom heard so many tributes from them after a sermon.

The way forward for him in Ireland appeared to be that of preacher of the Gospel.

A young Jesuit at the time observed that Fr Delaney was a little over medium height, had an erect 'military walk', and though he did not have a powerful voice as a preacher, he had a clear and carrying voice and good articulation.[9]

A country in celebration

On John's return journey from Ceylon, he spent some days in Palestine visiting places associated with the Gospel. The precise time of his arrival in Dublin is not clear. It seems likely that he would have aimed to be in Ireland for the much awaited Eucharistic Congress. The nation-wide devotion the Congress evoked presented a stark contrast to his experience of Catholicism in a multi-religion Ceylon.

The focal point for Jesuits in Dublin was the large Church of St Francis Xavier, Gardiner Street. There some of the official preparations for the Congress took place. There was a retreat for women, at which it proved impossible 'to give accommodation to the crowds that came to hear the sermons'. This was followed by a men's retreat during which 'there was not even standing room' in the church. During 1932, the whole country, save the unionist north, was caught up in celebration and religious observance.

A week in June was the highlight of the celebrations. If back in Ireland, it is likely that John Delaney would have followed the special ceremonies in Gardiner Street. On the Wednesday of the Congress week there was exposition of the Blessed Sacrament until midnight when Benediction was given. This was followed by a High Mass. 'The congregation filled the church, and outside people extended for about 100 yards on either side of the street'. Some 12,000 were said to have attended between day and evening. 'After Mass the entire congregation received Holy Communion.' During the week, ten altars were occupied for Mass from 5.00am to 10.00am. More than 60 Masses were celebrated each day in the church, some of them in different Eastern Rites.

At the great final Mass and ceremonies in the Phoenix Park, which was attended by an estimated million people, the Gardiner Street Church had a special section in which were accommodated '10,000 men and as many women'. In addition, the church's sodalities provided many of the stewards for the occasion. John, with his strong sense of organisation and management, which was to find scope in Gardiner Street in later years, could not but be impressed by 'the greatest good will to make things run smoothly' that was manifest on all sides. The Jesuit community's report

© The Father Browne Collection

O'CONNELL STREET AND O'CONNELL BRIDGE DURING CELEBRATIONS FOR THE EUCHARISTIC CONGRESS IN IRELAND, 1932

on the week observed: ' "Open house" was the order of the day, everyone being welcome to our table. The refectory reminded one of the Tower of Babel'.[10]

On the Mission Staff

Following some time recuperating, John was ready for occasional sermons. His prowess as a preacher was awarded on 10 October 1932, when he was entrusted with the Children of Mary retreat at Gardiner Street Church.[11] It proved a great success: 'the church was filled to the doors'.[12] The only other extant reference to pastoral activity on his part during 1932 was on 10 December. Then, at Belvedere College, he received thirty-four boys into the Sodality of Our Lady and was said to have preached 'a most instructive sermon'.[13]

The next year, however, was marked by an accumulation of work. He was appointed to the mission staff of the Irish Jesuit province, stationed at Rathfarnham Castle. The mission staff were a band of noted preachers, who travelled throughout Ireland conducting parish missions and directing a variety of retreats based on the Spiritual Exercises of St Ignatius Loyola, founder of the Jesuits.

The busiest times for the mission staff were during Lent, especially leading up to Easter, during the four weeks of Advent before Christmas and again shortly after Christmas. During the summer months there was a strong demand for eight day retreats from religious congregations, and during the school year there were requests for retreats of three days duration for boy and girl pupils. Delaney, as might be expected of a popular military chaplain, related well to men, but it soon became evident the he also was popular with women and had a good way with young people. A great amount of the work of the missioner was devoted to retreats for religious women and for schools. Convents were discerning about the kind of retreat director they wanted. They compared notes about directors, and frequently requested the Jesuit organiser of retreats for the particular person they sought for their retreat, sometimes proposing three names in order of preference.

Records of Delaney's retreats during 1933 are incomplete, yet from them one can get an idea of the nature and extent of his work at this early stage, and of the travelling involved. As he became better known, there would be a considerable increase in the number of his retreats. For 1933, the extant list of his retreat work is limited to the months March to December.

His first recorded retreat was for 19 to 28 March at the Brigidine Convent in Gloucester, England. He had been particularly asked for. The other retreats were in Ireland. From 27 April to 6 May he was at Cahiracon, County Clare, a convent serving the Chinese mission. The other venues can best be viewed in sequence:

22 June to 1 July: Convent of the Faithful Companions of Jesus, Limerick.
3 to 8 July: Loreto Convent, Rathfarnham, Dublin. Short retreats to 'Ladies, past pupils, and novices'.
6 to 15 August: Sisters of Charity, Stanhope Street, Dublin.
Date unknown, around this time: De La Salle Brothers, Waterford.
4 to 8 Sept: Retreat for Sodality of Our Lady, Glasthule, County Dublin
25 to 29 Sept: Retreat for boys, Mungret College, Limerick.
30 Sept to 2 Oct: Sisters of Charity, Dublin, retreat for blind persons.
3 to 7 Oct: Ballina, County Mayo, a school retreat.
7 to 11 Oct: Gortner Abbey, County Mayo, retreat for girl pupils.
28 Oct to 1 Nov: Sisters of St Louis, Kilkeel, County Mayo.
2 to 6 Nov: Gloucester Street, Dublin. A triduum of talks and prayer.
21 to 25 Nov: Sisters of Charity, Baldoyle, Dublin. A triduum, or 3 day Retreat.
4 to 8 Dec: Sisters of Charity, Benada Abbey, Sligo. A triduum.
11 to 15 Dec: Sisters of Charity, Stanhope Street.
15 to 19 Dec: Sisters of Charity, Temple Street, Dublin.
19 to 23 Dec: Loreto Sisters, Rathfarnham.
28 Dec to 1 Jan, 1934: Sisters of Mercy, St Mary of the Isles, Cork.

In the three-day retreats there were two to three talks each day, Mass with a homily, and confessions. In the eight-day retreats in those years, the director gave three or four talks each day, a homily during Mass each day, and was expected to be available for confessions and consultation.

It could be a heavy programme. It was to be heavier for John Delaney in 1934 as more convents and schools heard favourable reports about him.

In addition to his work on the mission team, he also had the distinction of being asked to preach at the solemn high Mass on 9 December, 1933, that marked the feast day of St Francis Xavier and the close of the historic Novena of Grace, which filled Gardiner Street Church night and morning for nine days. Notification of the Mass emphasised that the sermon would be by 'Rev. John J. Delaney SJ (Ceylon)'. His missionary experience was also to the fore during 1933 at his base, Rathfarnham Castle. As well as older Jesuits, the castle was occupied by 'Jesuit Juniors', younger men who studied for a BA at University College, Dublin. Amongst themselves, they ran a variety of societies. Some were active in the Xavier Mission Guild, which collected and sorted stamps in support of the Irish Jesuit mission in China and Hong Kong. In July 1933, Delaney was invited to speak to the guild, not on his missionary experience, but on his visit to the Holy Land on his way back from Ceylon. The rather bland account of the occasion remarked that he gave 'a very pleasing account of his visit to Palestine'.[14] He felt sympathy for the young men. The castle in the 1930s was a cold, draughty building, with inadequate heating, limited fare, and a confining, oppressive form of government. It was a difficult time generally for members of the Irish province, but Rathfarnham appears to have been particularly restrictive. For the mission staff, returning from a long mission or run of retreats, the ambience was less than welcoming.

In 1934, there was not only an increased demand on him for retreats, John's standing as a preacher was acknowledged by his being teamed with the most renowned preacher in the province at the time, Fr Patrick O'Donoghue. On Good Friday, they combined in preaching on the passion of Jesus Christ, from 12.00 noon to 3 o'clock in correspondence with the three hours agony of Jesus on the cross.[15] The occasion was always attended by a large congregation. On the first day of the New Year, 1935, John Delaney was called on for a short retreat. It was the start of another busy year. On 26 January, the minister, or Jesuit administrator of the house, commented: 'Fr Delaney left for Baldoyle for a week-end retreat, and after that Goresbridge [County Wexford], Armagh, Waterford'.[16] Thus it went, month after month, year after year.

St Francis Xavier church, Gardiner Street, Dublin
Crowds queuing for the Novena

Challenges of the War Years

The year 1941 was filled with testing experiences, some of which evoked memories of his own war years. On the night of 2 January, German planes dropped bombs on Rathdown Park and Donore Avenue in the vicinity of the castle. Some of the Juniors became quite nervous. Then, on 17 January there were heavy snow drifts, succeeded two nights later by 'an awful blizzard gale. Fr Delaney's window was blown in. People were kept awake for hours. Next day travel was deemed impossible. There was no university for the Juniors'. Much worse was yet to come. The presence of German planes led to anti-aircraft activity. Then, on the night of 30 to 31 May, German planes hovered over the North Strand Road area of Dublin from 12.30am to 2.00am. They dropped four high explosive bombs, one of them on John's home area, Charleville Mall. Twenty-eight people were killed, ninety were wounded, and 300 houses were damaged or destroyed. John's mother was long dead and it is not clear if any of his family still lived at 13 Charleville Mall. The area, however, was familiar to him and many people he knew had to have been affected by the bombing. A month later, on a somewhat lighter note, Irish army manoeuvres were centred on Rathfarnham Castle. It 'was attacked and taken'.

The following month, John Delaney had a further challenging surprise. On 31 July, the date on which changes were announced in the Irish province, he found himself moved from Rathfarnham Castle to Milltown Park. There was no let up, however, in the tempo of his mission work. He continued his constant regime of concentrated work, ever open to requests for talks and retreats. In the end it took an inevitable toll on his constitution.

In January 1943, the *Irish Province News* carried a report from Milltown Park that: 'Fr Delaney returned from a heavy mission in Rosscarbery [County Cork] to find that his tireless exertions during the past ten years had laid him low at last.'[17] It was April before the Milltown report was able to announce: 'We are glad to welcome back Fr Delaney after his long absence, and are glad also of the signs that he will be his old self soon, please God'. His provincial, Fr J.R. McMahon, decided, however, that John's health could no longer stand up to the demands on the mission staff. He 'transferred him to church work in Gardiner Street'.[18]

The Gardiner Street Years

Fr Delaney was already well known in Gardiner Street Church. In March 1943, prior to his appointment to Gardiner Street, he had preached each night of the Novena of Grace in honour of St Francis Xavier. As indicated earlier, the public following for the novena, in this church dedicated to the saint, was always immense. Crowds stood in the aisles and spread out into the street, where they remained, irrespective of the weather, until the conclusion of the service each night. It was no different during John's novena in 1943. 'Between 70 and 80 persons had to be attended by the Order of Malta'.[19]

The church served a congregation of all classes, from the wealthy to the very poor. In the confessional, in consultation and daily encounter, Delaney had ample opportunity to exercise the empathy and compassion remarked on during his years as chaplain. Gardiner Street Church in the 1940s, the years of 'the Emergency' and widespread privation, was frequented by many men, women and children who were poorly clad and under-nourished, and carried lice and the smells of neglect and deficient hygiene. John settled into the life of the church with renewed energy.

Shortly after his arrival permanently at Gardiner Street, he was appointed to succeed Fr William Gleeson as director of the Sodality of the Dublin Metropolitan Garda Siochána. The annual Garda retreat usually ended with a flourish. In 1943, 'on the closing day of the retreat, the Gards [sic] marched with the Depot band from Dublin Castle to Gardiner Street Church. About eighteen officers were entertained to tea by Fr Delaney at the close of the retreat'.[20] The next year, Delaney brought an additional solemnity to the close of the retreat. On the marchers' arrival at the church, at 3.45pm, they were met by the Fr Superior of the Jesuit community, Fr V. McGrath, Mr. Wolf, on behalf of the Dublin Metropolitan Garda (DMG), and Fr Delaney, and the salute was taken. Thereafter, the band received appropriate refreshments and, after the sodality ceremony in the church, the heads of the Garda were entertained. The following year, Delaney introduced a further improvement. After the close of the retreat, the Gardaí 'had tea, a concert, and a dance in the adjoining St Francis Xavier Hall'.[21] With his 'popular touch', cheerful manner, and genuine zeal, Delaney proved a popular director of the Garda Sodality.

This is, perhaps, an appropriate occasion to say a word about sodalities. No longer familiar in the twenty-first century, sodalities were very much a feature of Catholic life in the latter part of the 19th century and for much of the 20th century. They were confraternities or associations of men or women, who met at regular intervals for religious devotions and who frequently during their daily lives were required to say certain prayers, or give time to meditation, and were encouraged to be involved in some activity to benefit others, usually people who were sick or in special need. Sodalities played an important part in the lives of thousands of Irish men and women in the periods mentioned.

A special feature in Delaney's first year in Gardiner Street was that it was the centenary year of the Apostleship of Prayer organisation. Commemorations took place during 1943–1944. The major celebration, however, took place on 25 June 1944. That evening, in the presence of the new archbishop of Dublin, Dr John Charles McQuaid, John Delaney preached the sermon.[22] In his normal routine, he conducted both the Garda Sodality and a sodality for supplying altar requisites for poorly-off churches. Not content with that, he also took on the St Ignatius Sodality for men, and the direction of the women's sodality. On Sodality Day, 13 May 1945, he addressed the members of some 12 sodalities. Moreover, during Lent that year, he was the preacher chosen to give the Lenten Lectures each Sunday at 8.00pm The Lenten Lectures were another feature of Gardiner's Street Church that drew very large crowds. The theme of his lectures was, 'The Eternal Christ and the World of Today'.

Such undertakings were in addition to the daily rotas of work in a busy city church – with Masses, confessions (then a frequent practice), consultations in the parlours, and the meetings with the various societies attached to the church, such as, the Vincent de Paul Society and the St Joseph Young Priests Society (which prayed for and sought aid for young men wishing to be priests). As if there was no end to his energy, Delaney continued to give retreats to religious sisters, priests, teachers, and school pupils whenever the pressure of demand eased in his church work.

A feature of most of his years in Gardiner Street was his organisation of the annual 'Sale of Work in aid of the Jesuit mission to China'. The event, in 1945, ran from 8-10 November. The 'House History' reported:

> In previous years it had been held in the nearby St Francis Xavier's Hall. This year it was decided to hold it on a larger scale. It

GARDINER STREET 1949

Back Row: L to R

Frs Charles Moloney, Paddy Doherty, Hugh Kelly, Joe Corcoran, John Mac Sheehan, Michael Quinlan, Daniel Dargan, Joseph McAuliffe, John Delaney, Eddie Dillon, Jerry Higgins, Michael Kelly

Front Row: L to R

John Coyne (Socius), Michael Garahy, T. Byrne (Prov), Msgr (Papal Nuncio's See), Robert Tyndale (Sup), Papal Nuncio's Secretary, Mark Quigley, (Min) Gus O'Kelly

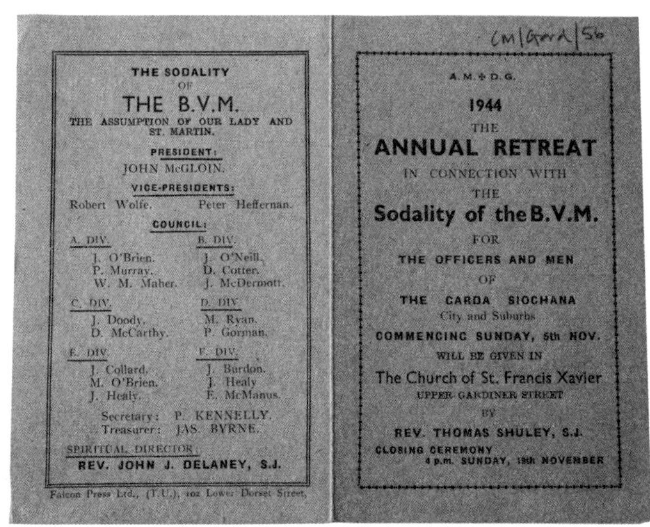

THE SODALITY
OF
THE B.V.M.
THE ASSUMPTION OF OUR LADY AND ST. MARTIN.

PRESIDENT:
JOHN McGLOIN.

VICE-PRESIDENTS:
Robert Wolfe. Peter Heffernan.

COUNCIL:

A. DIV.
J. O'Brien.
P. Murray.
W. M. Maher.

B. DIV.
J. O'Neill.
D. Cotter.
J. McDermott.

C. DIV.
J. Doody.
D. McCarthy.

D. DIV.
M. Ryan.
P. Gorman.

E. DIV.
J. Collard.
M. O'Brien.
J. Healy.

F. DIV.
J. Burdon.
J. Healy
E. McManus.

Secretary: P. KENNELLY.
Treasurer: JAS. BYRNE.

SPIRITUAL DIRECTOR:
REV. JOHN J. DELANEY, S.J.

Falcon Press Ltd., (T.U.), 102 Lower Dorset Street,

CM/Gard/56

A.M. ✠ D.G.

1944
THE
ANNUAL RETREAT
IN CONNECTION WITH
THE
Sodality of the B.V.M.
FOR
THE OFFICERS AND MEN
OF
THE GARDA SIOCHANA
City and Suburbs
COMMENCING SUNDAY, 5th NOV.
WILL BE GIVEN IN
The Church of St. Francis Xavier
UPPER GARDINER STREET
BY
REV. THOMAS SHULEY, S.J.
CLOSING CEREMONY
4 p.m. SUNDAY, 19th NOVEMBER

> was held in the Mansion House [the official residence of the Lord Mayor of Dublin]. All the sodalities were asked to co-operate, and it was voted a great success. Fr Delaney acted as secretary. The directors of the different sodalities either had a stall or helped in one way or another. Some weeks previously, Fr Delaney had a Whist Drive for the Garda Sodality in the Mansion House for the same purpose viz. the Jesuit Mission to China.

In 1946 the Sale of Work was so successful in the Mansion House, that Delaney decided that the following year they would use the largest room available, the very extensive Round Room.

The winter of 1946–1947 was intensely cold, especially from the end of January to the beginning of March 1947. There was also a shortage of fuel at this time, with the result that there was acute misery and suffering among the poor of the city. The church in Gardiner Street could not be heated. Great economy was exercised. The resourceful superior of the Jesuit community, Fr Robert Tyndall, succeeded in obtaining some tons of blocks of wood, which he distributed to the poor of the district.[23]

Delaney, as was his way, worked tirelessly during the years 1944–1946. It was observed that even during his community's villa, or summer holiday, he was away giving retreats. Once again, compounded perhaps by the intense cold of 1947, he fell seriously ill. He was sick for some months[24] and was hospitalised. On 19 December 1947 he returned to the community.[25] During 1948 he was back in action once more. That year he brought further life and enterprise to the Sale of Work in the Round Room of the Mansion House. 'The Garda's ceilidhe band and Miss Terry O'Connor's string orchestra played during the sale and were greatly appreciated. There was a new addition – the Cinema Workers' Sodality. They had a stall and a cinema show.' Moreover, the centre of the great room was occupied by a Chinese pagoda![26]

One of the functions undertaken by Delaney was the marshalling of the crowds at the special novenas and ceremonies. The greatest challenge occurred during December 1949. 'A special triduum [or three days of prayer] was held in the middle of December to commemorate the fourth centenary of St Francis Xavier's landing in Japan, in 1549.' The superior of the Gardiner Street community, Fr Tyndall, succeeded in obtaining from Rome a relic of the saint (his right arm) for the triduum. On the

SAINT FRANCIS XAVIER CHURCH, DECEMBER 1949

Above: the crowd inside the church for the special triduum to commemorate the fourth centenary of St Francis Xavier's landing in Japan, in 1549. Below: The crowd outside the church, because there was no more room inside.

final day of the celebration, the archbishop of Dublin presided at the Mass and the papal nuncio, Dr Ettore Felici, attended. In the evening, the papal nuncio gave the solemn Benediction. The newspapers, in text and photographs, recorded the occasion, particularly the vast crowds attending the ceremonies:

> It was estimated that about 100,000 people venerated the relics during the three days. Queues were formed after the last Mass and they were enormous. For example, on Sunday afternoon, the queue extended along Gardiner Street, Mountjoy Square, Belvedere Place, up and down Sherrard Street along North Circular Road to Dorset Street, up Dorset Street to Gardiner Street and a few hundred yards up Gardiner Street. The weather was fine but bitterly cold and some people had to wait in queue for three hours.[27]

In 1950 John Delaney was back to his former outpouring of energy. On Sodality Day, 14 May, he addressed over 2,000 members of sodalities. At the Novena of Grace it was recorded that:

> the crowds were as large as ever, even though the weather was dreadful on a few days – snow, sleet and cold. The loud speakers and additional accommodation helped greatly. During the very bad weather a great number were brought into the shelter of the house. But in spite of this, there were a great many who followed the devotions in the open, bitter air. Fr Delaney surpassed himself in the marshalling of the crowds. He was helped by the Gardaí and members of [other] sodalities.[28]

On Good Friday 1950 he had been one of the special preachers once again, and during the summer, with more zeal than judgement, he sacrificed his holiday in order to give two retreats in England. Towards the end of the year, he took 'charge of a very successful Sale of Work, in connection with which he organised a social [a dance] with the aid of the Garda Sodality'.

An indication of the size of the crowds attending Novena of Grace devotions was conveyed by a photograph in the *Irish Independent* of 14 March, 1952. It was the last night of the novena, and the photograph showed a great gathering packed closely together and all standing. It was

John Delaney's final year linked to the Novena. For many years he had conducted retreats in England, and he had also renewed contact with France by preaching and directing retreats there from time to time. During the summer of 1952, he went once again to England to conduct some retreats. 'Unfortunately, they were too much for him, and he spent a long period in hospital in Dublin on his return'.[29]

The closing years

Delaney never fully recovered. He went from hospital to Linden Convalescence Home, Blackrock, which was run by the Irish Sisters of Charity. At the Sale of Work that year his place was taken, with much success, by a Fr John McAvoy. Delaney was brought from the nursing home and 'made an appearance at the opening and got a great ovation'. He also managed to attend the exhibition of work for the poor churches.

Monday morning Newspapers. 12th Dec

33

Thousands Throng To Venerate Relic Of Jesuit Saint

THERE were unprecedented scenes of devotion at the Church of St. Francis Xavier, Gardiner St., Dublin, yesterday, the second day of the Triduum of public veneration of the relic of St. Francis Xavier. Over 40,000 people filed through the church to kiss or touch the reliquary enshrining the right forearm of the Saint. After Mass and Benediction the relic was exposed until 10 p.m.

At 6 p.m. up to 15,000 people were standing in a queue about a mile long. It stretched from the church doors down Gardiner St., along the north side of Mountjoy Square, down Belvedere Place, up one side of Sherrard St. and down the other, through the North Circular Rd. and Dorset St., and into Gardiner St. again.

Many of the people had come from the farthest counties, and since the Triduum began on Saturday many invalids travelled long distances to Dublin to pray for the intercession of the Saint. One of the first to kiss the reliquary after Mass yesterday was a young crippled boy who sat in the Vestry, where it was taken to him by Very Rev. R. Tyndall, S.J., Superior. The boy had come specially with his mother from the West of Ireland.

Public veneration began yesterday after the last Mass, sung by Rev. M. Quigley, S.J., after which Benediction was given by Father Tyndall. The large congregation joined in reciting the Prayer to St. Francis Xavier.

PERFECTLY PRESERVED

Father Tyndall then passed along the altar rails bearing the reliquary for the people to kiss. Through the glass front the Saint's hand could be clearly seen, perfectly preserved after 400 years. Relays of priests succeeded Father Tyndall in carrying the relic, but at 4 o'clock it was realised that the crowds were too great, and from that time it was left on the altar rail before the Tabernacle and each person laid his hand on it for a moment as he passed.

Preaching a sermon during the Mass, **Rev. Hugh Kelly,** S.J., said it was appropriate that in Ireland a great missionary people should welcome one of the greatest of the missionary saints, and they prayed that the occasion would be a source of national blessing, confirming them more strongly in their missionary vocation.

The circumstances in which the Saint's relic were brought to Japan this year were, perhaps, unique in the missionary annals of the church, he said. The visit inaugurated a new effort towards the conversion of that country, now humbled and defeated, but they hoped, disposed to the message of Christ. It was the greatest Christian missionary display ever seen there.

The ceremony at Hiroshima was particularly moving when they remembered how that city, the most flourishing Catholic centre in Japan, had been wiped out in one minute by the atomic bomb.

In its travels in Japan and through many other countries since it had been taken from the Gesu in Rome, the relic had been accorded the highest honours, both by Church and State.

The veneration will conclude at 9.30 to-night. The President and Mrs. O'Kelly will attend Solemn High Mass at which his Grace the Archbishop of Dublin, Most Rev. Dr McQuaid, will preside at 11 a.m. to-day.

At 5.15 p.m. his Excellency the Apostolic Nuncio, Most Rev. Dr Felici, will give Solemn Benediction.

Veneration of the relic of St. Francis Xavier at the Jesuit Church, Gardiner St., Dublin.

Irish Independent, Monday, December 12, 1949.

at 4 o'clock the

Meantime, the direction of the Garda Sodality was entrusted to Fr Tom O'Meara.[30]

The nature of John Delaney's protracted final illness has not been recorded. At first, as noted, he was able to attend occasional events. On 23 September, 1954, he celebrated his golden jubilee in the Society of Jesus. He appears to have attended events to mark the occasion. At the jubilee dinner, the vice-provincial, Fr John Coyne, read a letter of congratulations from the Father General of the Society and also from the provincial of the North Belgian province, of which Delaney was still a member. The superior of the Jesuit community in Gardiner Street, Fr Tim Mulcahy, paid tribute to Fr Delaney's work in the church, where he was known affectionately as the 'Great Marshall'. His calm and competent direction had meant so much for the orderly control of the great congregations who followed the annual Novenas of Grace as well as for the successful organisation of the Irish Jesuit Mission Week.

Fr Delaney received many congratulations from his Gardiner Street friends, particularly from the Garda Sodality and from the Sodality of Work for Poor Churches.[31] Among his visitors in 1955 was Cardinal Gracias, Archbishop of Bombay, who was on a visit to Ireland. He reminded John that he (John) had been present at his sacerdotal ordination.[32]

Fr John Delaney died a year later on 8 August, 1956. In its obituary, the *Irish Independent* reported:

> In Ireland Fr Delaney was a pre-eminent giver of retreats to religious communities. He gave many diocesan priests' retreats, and had a high reputation as a preacher. In Gardiner Street he was much sought after for spiritual direction both in and out of confession, and he was held in very high esteem by members of the Dublin Metropolitan Gardaí whose sodality he directed.[33]

Members of the Garda Sodality, under Superintendent T. O'Brien, provided a guard of honour at the funeral Mass. The chief mourners were mentioned as Mrs J. Brennan, England, and Rev. Sr Mary Oswald, Wales, John's sisters. Nieces and cousins also attended.[34] There was a large presence of clergy, and the Garda authorities were represented by the Garda Commissioner, Mr. D. Costigan, the Deputy Commissioner, Mr. G. Brennan, and Chief Superintendents M. Farrell and D. Connelly.[35]

John Delaney of the North Belgian Jesuit Province was buried in the Irish Jesuit plot in Glasnevin Cemetery on 10 August, 1956. None of his public obituaries made mention of the two most exciting periods in his life, the Easter Rising 1916, and his two years as military chaplain, 1917–1919, for which he was decorated and won the highest praise. His interest in, and his diary of the Rising was not widely known, and in the strong nationalist climate of the mid-1950s it was not politic to draw attention to service and decoration in the British army.

Reflection

Looking back over John Delaney's career, one is impressed by his single-minded determination, first to become a priest and then to achieve the joint goals of becoming a Jesuit and serving in Ceylon. During 1916 he was led by curiosity and determination to find out what was really happening. In the process he revealed nationalist sympathies and prejudice towards Protestants/unionists. In France and Flanders, 1917–1919, he served in the British army and displayed a driving desire and commitment to assist the men assigned to him, and to ensure, even at the cost of his own life, their spiritual and physical well being. In Ceylon, during his two sojourns, his enthusiasm, cheerfulness and capacity for work were manifested, as they were afterwards on the Irish Jesuit mission staff and in Gardiner Street Church. In his varied ministries he displayed the ability to relate to all classes and age groups. He was a man with authority, a gift for organisation and cheerful creativity, which won the co-operation of students, soldiers, the massed crowds at novenas in Gardiner Street and during Mission Week. In retrospect, however, he was also aware of his own shortcomings. Jesuits tend to be their own sharpest critics. His combination of zeal and great energy led, again and again, to his undertaking too much. It was as if he took too literally the words attributed to his Jesuit founder, St Ignatius of Loyola, 'to fight and not to count the cost', without taking into account his founder's emphasis on the importance of discernment and judgement. John Delaney pressed on inexorably, not seeking to know how much was too much, or that taking a holiday and pacing oneself were necessary for longer good health and effectiveness.

His final years must have been immensely frustrating. There was so much to be done, but he no longer had the energy nor the independent strength to undertake any apostolic work beyond praying for others at home and abroad.

Each death is unique, but he had helped so many young men to die on the mud-covered fields of Flanders that that must have been a strength to him in his own final days: days spent in a much kinder setting, and accompanied by the prayers and presence of fellow Jesuits and nursing sisters. And through all his life there had run a deep personal devotion to Jesus Christ as his leader and friend, and a trust that when his hour came there would be no need to explain anything, that, in the comforting adapted words of a distinguished Irish priest poet, he would row across the short channel to the mainland

And find Him standing
Where the white shingle
Drops deeply into sea

Waiting to gather him
Under His russet coat.[36]

NOTES

1. Belgian Jesuit Archives. BE 943 855 – 1515 – 11704 – 001ff
2. *Mungret Annual*, Jan 1926, pp. 323-4
3. *Irish Province News*, April 1944, pp. 725-6
4. *Irish Independent*, 9 Aug 1956, p. 10
5. *The Aloysian*, 1956–7, p. 117
6. *Mungret Missionary Magazine*, 1929, produced by Apostolic School, p. 26
7. *The Aloysian*, idem, pp. 269-71
8. 'Sodalists' – those received into membership of a sodality or confraternity under the patronage of Mary, Mother of Jesus, and involving certain daily prayer and social activity.
9. Interview with Fr Kevin Laheen SJ.
10. *Irish Province News* (IPN), 1932, on the Eucharistic Congress
11. Journal of the Rector, Gardiner Street, 10 Oct. 1932
12. IPN Jan 1933
13. Idem, April 1933
14. Idem, July 1933
15. Irish Jesuit Archives (IJA), Minister's Journal, Rathfarnham, 30 March 1934
16. Idem, 26 Jan 1935
17. IPN, 1943, p. 678
18. Idem, Oct 1943, p. 764
19. IJA, *Historia Domus* (History of the House), Gardiner St, 1942–43

20. Idem.
21. Idem, 1945–46
22. Idem, 1885–1954
23. Idem, 1946–47
24. Idem, 1947–48
25. Journal of the Rector, Gardiner Street, 31 Dec 1921 – 6 Feb 1948
26. *Hist. Domus,* Gardiner Street 1948
27. Idem, 1949–50
28. Idem, 1950–51
29. Idem, 1952–53
30. Idem.
31. IPN, Jan 1955, p. 5
32. *Irish Independent,* 9 Aug 1956
33. Idem.
34. Irish Press, 11 Aug 1956. Nieces were named as: Mrs C Leonard, Mrs J Kenny, Mrs C Doyle. Cousins mentioned were: Mr. Mrs WEF Manning, Mr. Mrs P Hughes, Mrs M Doyle, Mrs J Joyce, Mr. W Lysaght, Mrs M Brennan.
35. Idem, 11 Aug 1956.
36. Pádraig Daly, OSA, "The Resurrection" cit in John F Deane. *The Words of Love: incarnation, ecology and poetry.* (Dublin: Columba, 2010), p. 349

Index